Digital
Entreprene

Technology has enabled a new age of entrepreneurship as entrepreneurs find digital tools that enable new ventures to exploit commercial opportunities around the world. This textbook provides students with expert guidance on using technology platforms to start new ventures.

With an award-winning approach, the author guides readers through the process of a lean startup, taking a "digital first" approach to entrepreneurship. Students using the book will emerge with enhanced understanding of different digital business models, analytical skills for digital ventures, and the confidence to move from prototype to product.

Online resources such as slides, a sample syllabus, and exercises encourage the classroom to become an interactive and dynamic space.

Jonathan P. Allen is a Professor at the School of Management, University of San Francisco, USA.

'At last, a textbook we can use to teach our students digital entrepreneurship!'

—*Clyde Eiríkur Hull, Professor, Rochester Institute of Technology, USA*

Digital
Entrepreneurship

Jonathan P. Allen

Routledge
Taylor & Francis Group

NEW YORK AND LONDON

First published 2019
by Routledge
52 Vanderbilt Avenue, New York, NY 10017

and by Routledge
2 Park Square, Milton Park, Abingdon, Oxon, OX14 4RN

Routledge is an imprint of the Taylor & Francis Group, an informa business

© 2019 Taylor & Francis

Library of Congress Cataloging-in-Publication Data
A catalog record for this title has been requested

ISBN: 978-1-138-58367-2 (hbk)
ISBN: 978-1-138-58369-6 (pbk)
ISBN: 978-0-429-50656-7 (ebk)

Typeset in Helvetica
by Apex CoVantage, LLC

Visit the eResources: www.routledge.com/9781138583696

MIX
Paper from
responsible sources
FSC
www.fsc.org   FSC™ C013985

Printed in the United Kingdom
by Henry Ling Limited

Contents

Preface
Entrepreneurship in a Digital World

Do you want to start something new? Do you have an idea for a better product, or a better way of doing things? Do you want to be the founder of a business that will serve others, achieve your goals, and reflect your values?

If so, you're not alone. Interest in entrepreneurship has probably never been greater. Some entrepreneurs are forced into action by circumstance, but for others entrepreneurship is the pursuit of a lifelong dream, an attempt at a more meaningful and satisfying life. If the goal includes making the world a better place, entrepreneurship is one of the most important and powerful mechanisms for changing a world that is increasingly driven by business.

The digital transformation of business and society is changing many things, and entrepreneurship is no exception. The purpose of this book is to introduce this emerging new world of digital entrepreneurship by doing it. Our goal is to empower you, the reader, to take advantage of the power of new technology for entrepreneurship, and to navigate its new risks. People born since the birth of the commercial Internet have been called 'digital natives', and we think that new businesses in this era will be 'digital natives' as well.

This book doesn't assume any previous technical background. One of the best ways to learn entrepreneurship is through real-world experience, and digital entrepreneurship makes creating new products and services and getting them in the hands of potential customers that much easier. The learning process used in this book is to help you create a new digital business of your own. The book will guide you step by step through a simple version of the digital entrepreneurship process: choosing a digital business idea, building a prototype, testing the business idea on potential customers, and launching the business.

This book can be used as a stand-alone introduction to entrepreneurship, or as a supplement to a traditional entrepreneurship course looking to update its content for the digital era, and add more hands-on project work. The method of teaching digital entrepreneurship used in this book was developed primarily for undergraduate and masters' business students, but more technical students and liberal arts students have also used the course material to build their entrepreneurial skills.

Digital technology makes creating a new business venture easier in many ways, and this book will help the reader take advantage of those changes. But the digital world also creates new challenges, such as competing for online attention and keeping new businesses secure. In addition to creating many practical new entrepreneurial tools, the digital world also impacts the theoretical side of entrepreneurship, increasing the importance of issues such as data, user experience, and experimentation. Strategies, as well as tactics and tools, are changing.

The first phase in creating a new digital business is to identify a new opportunity. Chapters 1, 2, and 3 introduce the new opportunities created by digital technology and should help you choose a new digital business idea to prototype and test. The end product of the first phase is a digital business design, a high-level overview of the main aspects of a digital business.

The next phase is to prototype the digital business design. Chapters 4–7 show how to create a surprisingly sophisticated web prototype using freely available software and inexpensive Internet technology, how to add attractive content, how to create a look and feel for a prototype, and how to add new functionality that is appropriate for a new business idea. Chapters 8 and 9 show how to collect data about a prototype by using web analytics technology to create and track business goals. The end product of the second phase is a working prototype that is ready to be tested on potential customers.

The third phase is to test the prototype. The goal in this phase is to learn quickly from experience, and either make a digital business idea more effective, or change it. Chapter 10 shows how to do usability testing to improve customer experience. Chapter 11 introduces customer acquisition in the digital world, using search, social media, and other online channels. Chapter 12 discusses how to improve a business design, by analyzing customer data, and by running experiments to maximize the chances of achieving business goals.

The final phase is to launch a new digital business. Chapter 13 covers four of the major issues faced by new digital businesses as they start and grow: legal and regulatory compliance, security and disaster recovery, technical performance, and custom development. As your new digital business emerges, it is an opportunity to reconsider other classic issues in entrepreneurship such as creativity, business planning, marketing, team building, and financing.

A healthy economy, like a healthy community, invites as many people as possible to participate, contribute, and share in its success. Entrepreneurship and new ventures can do much more than provide financial success for founders and new products for consumers. Entrepreneurship at its best keeps an economy vibrant and diverse, reflecting the values of the people who depend on it, and addressing their ever-changing needs.

We believe that digital entrepreneurship can make new venture creation more inclusive and democratic. But digital technology alone will not make these changes happen automatically. It will require the hard work and vision of entrepreneurs to realize technology's potential to make things better. I hope this book helps.

Jonathan P. Allen
San Francisco, California, USA

Digital Entrepreneurship

New Opportunities and Challenges

Highlights

Chapter 1 introduces the new world of digital entrepreneurship.

- Entrepreneurship is being changed by the digital transformation of business and society. We call this *digital entrepreneurship*.

- The digital era is changing entrepreneurship by reducing barriers to new venture creation, and by creating new areas of opportunity.

- The digital era also creates new entrepreneurial challenges, such as competing for online attention, and keeping new businesses secure.

- Digital entrepreneurship offers the promise of empowering people to do more in the world, by making new venture creation more inclusive and democratic.

- Digital technology does not automatically create a better world. It will take the hard work of entrepreneurs to realize the potential of digital technology for not just creating wealth, but for keeping economies vibrant, diverse, and reflective of the values of the people they serve.

What Is Digital Entrepreneurship?

Imagine being able to reach thousands, millions, or billions of potential customers, anywhere in the world at almost any time, with technology so cheap that many companies give it away for free. Imagine being able to create new products and services on a personal device, then delivering them with the same global reach and speed as the largest companies. Imagine being able to choose from a variety of ways to generate revenue for your business, from advertising and subscriptions, to matchmaking, sales, or even donations and crowdfunding. It sounds like an entrepreneur's dream world.

The purpose of this book is to provide a path to getting started in this new era of entrepreneurship. We call this world *digital entrepreneurship*, or entrepreneurship that is affected by, or takes advantage of, the digital transformation of business and society. Many of the fundamental issues of entrepreneurship still apply in this new world: cultivating an entrepreneurial mindset; identifying good opportunities; building a great team; knowing your customers; fulfilling legal obligations; and raising capital, to name just a few. Yet each one of these areas is changed by the digital world; sometimes subtly, sometimes more fundamentally. With digital entrepreneurship, we are interested in the fundamental changes that a fully connected, always-on, digital society brings to all business activities, independent of any specific new technological breakthrough [1].

Using the classic definition of entrepreneurship as starting or owning a business venture, digital entrepreneurship changes things in at least three ways: by reducing the barriers to starting a new business, by creating new opportunities for entrepreneurial activity, and by raising new challenges to launching a new business that never existed before.

More recently, the definition of entrepreneurship has expanded beyond starting a new business to include any situation where a risk-taker identifies and exploits an opportunity to create something new that has value and will endure. In this new view, entrepreneurs seek to find, develop, and combine existing resources in original and more valuable ways when many of these resources may be outside of their personal control [2].

The digital world offers a vast universe of new resources for entrepreneurs to take advantage of, from exponentially growing collections of open data, content, code, and services to the online contributions of users and communities around the world. The digital world also provides novel ways of recombining these resources. For example, a small business site can tap into huge advertising networks, AI-based chatbots, global freelancers, or language translation with just a few clicks or a few lines of code.

The most effective ways of learning entrepreneurship all involve real-world experience. Starting a new business in the digital world is now within everyone's grasp. Digital technology is transforming the process of getting a live product or service in front of a real customer.

Reducing Barriers to Entrepreneurship in the Digital Era

The new digital capabilities at our fingertips can appear overwhelming. The power of the cloud, big data, social media, mobile technology, and artificial intelligence have all increased dramatically while costs have plummeted. Digital hardware, software, networks, and storage all continue to improve their capabilities at near exponential rates.

So it should not be surprising that digital technology might encourage entrepreneurship. An online business site that can sell to thousands of customers can be launched in minutes (with some practice!) for the price of a good cup of coffee. A growing business can use cloud-based services to scale up to millions of customers, by renting almost unlimited digital capabilities by the hour.

Reducing barriers to entrepreneurship is important to the many people who want to become entrepreneurs at some point in their lives. In the US, 65% of adults say entrepreneurship is a more prestigious occupation than being a business executive or a banker, and 75% of parents would encourage their child to pursue entrepreneurship [3]. Two thirds of the world's population have positive attitudes towards entrepreneurship [4], with over 40% of people seeing opportunities to start their own company. Today in the US 0.31% of the population become entrepreneurs monthly—that's over three quarters of a million new entrepreneurs every month [5]. And the rate is even higher in some other countries.

While the majority of entrepreneurs have traditionally started later in life after taking years to accumulate experience, create a network, and build their savings, today's youth are thinking about entrepreneurship earlier. In one survey, 62% of millennials said they had considered starting their own business [6]. The global GEM survey finds that age 25–34 is now the peak period for entrepreneurship. Yet a lack of knowledge, lack of experience, and fear of the consequences of failure keep many from pursuing their dream.

Here are some of the ways that barriers to entrepreneurship are being reduced in the digital era: by making entrepreneurship faster, cheaper, and easier, with new possibilities for collaboration, and by making entrepreneurship more effective.

Faster Entrepreneurship

A typical timeline for starting a new local business might finalize a business idea in month one, then start to develop a physical location or online store around month six [7]. A simple digital business, even one with customized products or content, and backed by a shopping cart or revenue generating advertisements, can be started in an afternoon. Faster startup encourages digital entrepreneurs to experiment and learn quickly. A new business idea can be tested and refined at the same time as the business is built, rather than waiting for a fully formed business to be launched before an idea can be tested. Faster launch allows digital entrepreneurs to test an idea during a vacation, summer, or a 'side hustle' without having to give up their regular career and obligations. Digital entrepreneurs can keep their 'day jobs' until a fast business launch proves itself.

Cheaper Entrepreneurship

In the US, 62% of millennials have considered starting their own business, but with a median net worth under $7,000 USD and median debt of over $45,000 USD [6], they often lack the means to do so. The digital world is filled with many free or cheap digital tools for communication, storage, site building, payments, invoicing, and consumer surveys [8]. Digital platforms for buying and selling are widespread, and have low startup costs (such as eBay, Amazon, Etsy, and Shopify). The major cloud computing providers (including Amazon, Google, and Microsoft) all offer free levels of service. Digital marketing through social media and online advertisements offer low startup costs. Crowdfunding sites are a cheap way to raise early funds. Compared to an average startup cost of half a million USD in the first dot com era, to around 50 thousand USD at the beginning of the Web. 2.0 era, the cost of digital business launch is now approaching zero [9]. Lower costs have allowed some startups to 'bootstrap' themselves through crowdfunding and personal funds, postponing more formal fundraising until much later [10].

Easier Entrepreneurship

Coding, data analysis, and other technical skills in the digital era can be challenging to master. Do digital entrepreneurs have to become master coders or data scientists? Not necessarily, especially at the beginning. Many of the tools of digital entrepreneurship have become vastly easier to use. Setting up an online store or starting an online advertising campaign requires no specific coding expertise. Sites can be built and maintained with easy-to-use software. Customer data can be collected and analyzed with web analytics. And many digital services and resources can be connected together in almost endless combinations, a phenomena referred to as the 'generativity' of digital technology [11]. This book is designed to help you develop your digital entrepreneurship skills regardless of technology background.

New Possibilities for Collaboration

The Internet allows for unprecedented access to millions or billions of potential customers around the world, but the collaboration possibilities of digital entrepreneurship extend beyond reaching customers. Customers now have opportunities to contribute new ideas, become funders, or even participate in the creation of new products and services. Entrepreneurs can use powerful tech platforms, or 'digital entrepreneurial ecosystems' [12], to communicate, work with, and sell to others.

Digital entrepreneurship can take advantage of access to potential partners and suppliers around the world. While entrepreneurship has traditionally focused on individuals as creative risk takers, the wider reach of digital entrepreneurship opens new possibilities for sharing the risk and creative burdens with others [11].

More Effective Entrepreneurship

Faster, cheaper, and easier entrepreneurship with new collaboration possibilities opens the door for more effective entrepreneurship, if effectiveness is defined as better learning and decision making about the exploitation of an entrepreneurial opportunity. Digital entrepreneurship can experiment faster, learn faster, and act on that knowledge faster. Many of the biggest perceived barriers to entrepreneurship have to do with a perceived lack of competency, support, and experience, leading to a fear of the negative consequences of failure [13], particularly for people from traditionally under-represented backgrounds in entrepreneurship. Increasing the probability of success or reducing the consequences of failure could be a game changer.

By reducing the barriers to entrepreneurship, the digital era allows for more emphasis on business exploration rather than business planning. Digital entrepreneurship opens the possibility of what is known as an 'effectuation' process [14]. Effectuation is the use of whatever resources are at hand as a starting point and building from there, rather than starting from a business plan with large and complex resource needs that an entrepreneur will struggle to obtain. The 'lean startup' movement, popular in the digital technology startup world, sees early stage entrepreneurship as an experimental or learning process that searches quickly and cheaply for a new business idea that works [15, 16].

New Digital Opportunities: Experimentation, Data, and Scale

Digital entrepreneurship not only makes existing forms of entrepreneurship easier to try, it also opens up new areas of entrepreneurial opportunity. Here we highlight three new areas of opportunity: experimentation, data, and scale. The digital world allows entrepreneurs to experiment with new business ideas more quickly and cheaply, using simple prototypes as fast learning tools. Digital entrepreneurship makes the capture and use of unique data a new area of opportunity, allowing entrepreneurs to offer more valuable and better-targeted products and services. The globally connected digital world provides entrepreneurs with a whole new set of opportunities to take advantage of the Internet and personal devices and to adjust the size of a new business dynamically as new opportunities arise.

Each area of digital opportunity raises a new question that entrepreneurs can ask themselves:

- Where can I quickly and cheaply create a simple prototype of my business idea to learn what works, and rapidly improve? (Experimentation)

- What unique data will I be able to generate or acquire and how will it help me serve people better? (Data)

- How can I start my business focused on a highly specialized niche, then adjust my size up and down as needed? (Scale)

Experimentation

The digital world allows an entrepreneur to start with a simple prototype of a business. These prototypes, also known as MVPs (Minimum Viable Products), are deliberately kept as simple as possible so that entrepreneurs can learn what works with minimal startup cost. A deliberately simple prototype can be changed (or abandoned) more easily. The prototype is an attempt to surface assumptions about a new business, measure these assumptions, and test them in ways that are actionable. Digital products and services particularly benefit from an experimental approach because of their inherent openness; digital products are easier to change, update, and recombine than their physical counterparts [11].

Even the largest digital startups, such as Facebook, began with simplified versions and provided very limited functionality for a small set of initial users. One of the fastest digital startups to achieve $1 billion USD in revenue began with a WordPress site and PDFs of pizza coupons, while a shoe retailer that became one of Amazon's largest acquisitions began by taking shoe orders in blog comments [15]. The world's largest classified ad site, Craigslist, began as a small email newsletter, and a site in the global top 50 for web traffic, IMDB, began as a list posted on an electronic bulletin board by a movie fan.

Simple digital MVPs allow an entrepreneur to target a small set of eager customers first, rather than waiting for the development of a blockbuster product that will be launched to a mass market. Experimentation allows the digital entrepreneur to look for disruption or change opportunities in just about any aspect of business and life, not only in huge existing markets. A digital entrepreneur might even use a 'concierge MVP', which simulates a fully automated service at first through manual activity. For example, a grocery picking and delivery service might receive orders as a comment or a simple form, rather than a fully coded app, and the founders might go to the grocery store, pick up the food, and deliver the items themselves for the first few customers. When the business concept proves itself and more is known about customer needs, then the entrepreneurs can invest in further technology development.

A more experimental approach raises concerns for some entrepreneurs. Some worry about launching 'low quality' products, but as pointed out by the 'lean startup' movement, quality is impossible to define until customers and their needs are known. Most of today's famous digital startups begin with low quality products (and some would argue the tradition continues!). Other entrepreneurs are concerned that someone else will steal their idea if it is released as an experiment. The typical response to this concern is along the lines of 'ideas are cheap'. Ries suggests the following experiment: go to a company and try to have someone steal your idea—offer them your idea for free and see if they will launch a product based on it. Most likely they will not take up your generous offer. According to the experimental approach, being first or having a unique idea is not the path to entrepreneurial success. "The only way to win is to learn faster than everyone else". [15]

If anything, the experimental approach requires entrepreneurs to develop a unique combination of perseverance and flexibility. Fortunately, digital entrepreneurs can make the difficult decision to 'pivot', or change their digital business idea, with the aid of customer data and experimental results.

Data

For digital entrepreneurs, the ability to capture and use a unique data set is a powerful new area of business opportunity. Every action taken on a digital product or service leaves a data trace, and this data can provide powerful insights into exactly how products and services should evolve to create even more value for customers.

One major advantage that digital companies have is their unique data on customer behavior. An entertainment platform like Netflix has an incredible data set on viewer preferences that can be used to guide their decisions about which content to invest in. Social media platforms such as Facebook have unbelievably detailed data about which content will create more likes, shares, and advertisement views. Their engagement data can be used to customize what each user will be shown in their news feed. A search engine such as Google has detailed data about the information customers are searching for, which can be used to decide which information sources and advertisements to display that will be the most relevant for customers (or maximize advertising revenue for publishers).

Digital entrepreneurs look for unique data opportunities everywhere. A local business might be able to obtain unique information about people in a certain neighborhood, for example about local food tastes or how receptive locals are to a particular discount or special offer. A niche content business devoted to discussing an obscure science fiction show might find itself with the best data in the world about which character in that fictional universe is most likely to drive T-shirt sales. Anywhere there is an opportunity to make products or services better, there is the possibility of a unique set of data which would make even a small startup the most knowledgeable company in the world about a particular topic or decision. And where there is good data, there is an opportunity to use an algorithm, or automated decision method, to further the advantage a startup might have in providing more valuable products and services.

Scale

In the non-digital world, changing the size of a business is a major effort. Expanding from a single restaurant to a second or third location can take months or years and require significant new hiring and capital. Digital entrepreneurs have the luxury of being able to start small, yet grow quickly.

At its smallest, a digital business can focus on serving an incredibly specialized niche, locally or around the world. The Internet can support a business devoted to serving 150 passionate fans of a particular lizard variety, or to a specialized e-book series for followers of a lower-division French football team. While many digital businesses will likely remain small, there are examples of small businesses with only a few employees quickly growing to support millions of customers, as in the case of Instagram. New digital businesses can take advantage of existing platforms like social media and search to quickly build audiences and provide new services that benefit members of already existing massive communities.

Besides enabling every size of business, the digital world makes it easier to change the size of a business to fit the opportunity. Through cloud computing, new digital businesses can easily scale up or scale down the amount of technology they need within minutes, renting new capabilities by the hour if, one afternoon, a custom T-shirt becomes a national bestseller; then shutting those capabilities down again when sales subside later in the week.

The ability to easily scale up or down argues for a strategy of focusing on the most specialized niche possible at first, learning how to build a viable new business around that opportunity, then expanding as new related opportunities are found. Digital entrepreneurs are always on the lookout for a new customer need that might have traditionally been perceived as too small or limited in scope, but now can be used as a launching point for a new venture that can adjust its size up or down as it learns more about the viability of a business idea.

New Digital Challenges: Security, Privacy, and Competing for Attention

The new world of digital entrepreneurship brings new threats and challenges as well as opportunities. A traditional entrepreneur starting a new dry-cleaning business or restaurant probably doesn't have to turn their business upside down every time the European Union updates their privacy regulations, or defend themselves against foreign criminals trying to break into their stores multiple times per day.

Digital entrepreneurs have to deal with this instantly globalized complexity and more. They must find a way to work in the shadow of the largest and most powerful technology companies in the world, yet effectively compete with them at the same time. And digital entrepreneurs have to stay on top of a turbocharged social media environment where comments, images, or tweets can go viral at any time and make or break careers.

In this introduction, we briefly mention three examples of the new challenges for digital entrepreneurs: keeping a digital business secure from attack, maintaining privacy and consumer trust, and capturing consumer attention in a very crowded digital marketplace.

Security

Online attempts to break into even the smallest businesses have become routine. If you keep track of the unsuccessful login attempts at any new digital business, you will quickly see how many attackers are trying to break every single day. Estimates vary, but somewhere in the range of 15–50% of all businesses are subject to a serious digital security incident each year [17]. Larger companies are more likely to be attacked, but security breaches are costlier as percentage of revenue for smaller companies.

The major objective of attackers is either to gain unauthorized access or deny you access to your own business, or both. Infecting your business with viruses or malware is still the most common method of attack, and ransomware attacks are on the rise. Digital businesses can also become the target of a denial of service attack or be used as part of an attack on others. Criminals can attack by taking advantages of errors in software code, especially before they are known and corrected, and through 'social engineering' such as phishing attacks that obtain passwords via fraudulent sites.

Because software can fundamentally never be error free for any real-life application, and people are only willing to do so much additional work to maximize safety, digital businesses will never be completely secure. All digital entrepreneurs can do is reduce the odds of attack and be ready to recover at a moment's notice if an attack is successful. Tools and strategies are available, but they require constant vigilance.

Privacy

Digital businesses can and often do collect detailed personally identifiable information. While consumers have largely become resigned to sharing this information, almost 50% of people have stopped themselves from performing an action online because of a lack of trust [17]. Detailed consumer information in the wrong hands can lead to more serious problems of identity theft and fraud.

Privacy regulations are increasing in complexity. For example, recent changes in EU law give businesses an obligation to ask for explicit consent before collecting any personally identifiable information and give consumers the right to have all personal information removed from a business at any time. These laws require digital entrepreneurs to structure their technology in ways that meet these changing requirements, and to maintain people and processes to manage privacy requests.

Competing for Attention

With easier access to customers in the digital world comes increased competition for attention and visibility. It is no exaggeration to say there are billions of social media accounts, hundreds of millions of web sites, and millions of mobile apps all competing for consumer attention. And once attention is earned, maintaining a following requires constant care and feeding.

Compared to the advertising and promotion choices of traditional entrepreneurs, it can feel overwhelming for digital entrepreneurs to have to master the intricacies of search engine optimization or crack the mystery of creating viral content just to fulfill the simple business need of getting customers in the door. This complexity can be an advantage for the new digital entrepreneurs who know how to focus and position their offerings. But gaining customers in the digital world sometimes feels more like a long-term community-building process than running a business, a feeling that can be both exhilarating and exhausting at the same time.

The Bigger Picture: Making Entrepreneurship Inclusive

Digital entrepreneurship offers the possibility of empowering people to do more in the world by making new venture creation more democratic and inclusive. Entrepreneurship is believed to have many individual and societal benefits, which is why so many countries around the world are promoting entrepreneurship and entrepreneurship education. In parts of the world where populations have been excluded from entrepreneurship for cultural reasons, the digital world can help overcome barriers to the mechanics of entrepreneurship such as filling in forms and obtaining licenses. More importantly, digital entrepreneurship can take advantage of new forms of trust building, such as an online presence and social media activity, that allow underrepresented groups to connect to investors and customers outside of traditional networks of power and influence [18].

Entrepreneurship adds a healthy dynamism to economies, as well as diversity. There is concern in the developed economies about declining rates of entrepreneurship—new firm formation rate in the US has fallen by half in the last 30 years—combined with a concentration of market power in a few 'superstar' firms [19]. The digital world has not been immune from this trend. As of this writing, seven of the ten largest companies in the world by market capitalization are digital giants: Apple, Google, Microsoft, Amazon, and Facebook, plus the Chinese giants Tencent and Alibaba.

Digital technology by itself will not automatically create a better world. The digital technology industries have so far been associated as much with wealth concentration as democratization [20], and technology businesses have not had the best record of attracting and retaining a diverse workforce, management, or set of investors. The online world is far from immune to gender, ethnic, ability, and other forms of exclusion, even for entrepreneurs [21]. For digital entrepreneurship to be a positive force it needs to be an inclusive one, inviting as many as possible to be a part of the digital economy of the future. It will take the hard work of entrepreneurs to realize the potential of digital technology for not just creating wealth but for keeping economies vibrant, diverse, and reflective of the values of the people they serve.

Additional Resources

www.inc.com/online-business—general articles about
    Internet entrepreneurship.
www.inc.com/technology—news about technology
    developments in entrepreneurship.

www.entrepreneur.com/topic/online-business—general
articles about Internet entrepreneurship.
www.entrepreneur.com/topic/technology—news about
technology developments in entrepreneurship.

Exercises

1.1. Describe an idea you had in the past for a new product or service that you were *not* able to pursue. Which of the barriers mentioned in the chapter most prevented you from pursuing this idea?

1.2. For the preceding idea, what would be an MVP (digital or not) that you could create to test it?

1.3. Give an example of unique data that you might be able to collect better than anyone else. How could you use it to better target a product or service? What specialized niche of customers might it apply to?

1.4. Give an example of a company that has successfully earned your trust online. What information are you willing to share with them that you will not share with other businesses. Why are they effective?

1.5. Give an example of how a company has successfully won your attention online. Why are they effective?

1.6. Describe your current skill level with digital technology for business. Which technologies do you have experience with? Which aspects of digital technology are you excited to learn more about? Which aspects seem intimidating?

1.7. Do you think that entrepreneurship has a role to play in making a better world? Or is it mostly about money and lifestyle?

References

[1] F. Giones and A. Brem, "Digital Technology Entrepreneurship: A Definition and Research Agenda," *Technology Innovation Management Review*, vol. 7, no. 5, pp. 44–51, 2017.

[2] T. R. Eisenmann, "Entrepreneurship: A Working Definition," *Harvard Business Review*, pp. 1–2, 2013.

[3] A. Birth. *2 in 3 Americans See Entrepreneurship as a Prestigious Occupation*. (2016), available: www.theharrispoll.com/business/6-in-10-americans-say-chef-is-a-prestigious-occupation.html. [Accessed: June 23, 2017].

[4] GEM Consortium. *Gem 2017/2018 Global Report*. (2018), available: www.gemconsortium.org/report/50012. [Accessed: May 30, 2018].

[5] Kauffman Foundation. *The Kauffman Index*. (2017), available: www.kauffman.org/kauffman-index/. [Accessed: June 26, 2017].

[6] Economic Innovation Group. *The Millennial Economy: National Public Opinion Survey September 2016*. (2016), available: www.eig.org/wp-content/uploads/2016/09/EY-EIG-Millennial-Poll-Findings.pdf. [Accessed: June 26, 2017].

[7] S. Belew and J. Elad, *Starting an Online Business All-in-One for Dummies*. Hoboken, NJ: John Wiley & Sons, 2017.

[8] R. Stim and L. Guerin, *Running a Side Business: How to Create a Second Income*. Berkeley, CA: Nolo, 2009.

[9] B. Feld and S. Wise, *Startup Opportunities: Know When to Quit Your Day Job*. Hoboken, NJ: John Wiley & Sons, 2017.

[10] J. Del Rey. *The Rise of Giant Consumer Startups That Said No to Investor Money*. (2018), available: www.recode.net/2018/8/29/17774878/consumer-startups-business-model-native-mvmt-tuft-needle. [Accessed: August 31, 2018].

[11] S. Nambisan, "Digital Entrepreneurship: Toward a Digital Technology Perspective of Entrepreneurship," *Entrepreneurship Theory and Practice*, vol. 41, no. 6, pp. 1029–1055, 2017.

[12] F. Sussan and Z. J. Acs, "The Digital Entrepreneurial Ecosystem," *Small Business Economics*, vol. 49, no. 1, pp. 55–73, 2017.

[13] R. S. Shinnar, O. Giacomin, and F. Janssen, "Entrepreneurial Perceptions and Intentions: The Role of Gender and Culture," *Entrepreneurship Theory and Practice*, vol. 36, no. 3, pp. 465–493, 2012.

[14] J. T. Perry, G. N. Chandler, and G. Markova, "Entrepreneurial Effectuation: A Review and Suggestions for Future Research," *Entrepreneurship Theory and Practice*, vol. 36, no. 4, pp. 837–861, 2012.

[15] E. Ries, *The Lean Startup: How Today's Entrepreneurs Use Continuous Innovation to Create Radically Successful Businesses*. New York: Crown Business, 2011.

[16] X. Yang, S. L. Sun, and X. Zhao, "Search and Execution: Examining the Entrepreneurial Cognitions Behind the Lean Startup Model," *Small Business Economics*, pp. 1–13, 2018.

[17] *OECD* Publishing, *Oecd Digital Economy Outlook 2017*. Paris: OECD Publishing, 2017.

[18] M. McAdam, C. Crowley, and R. T. Harrison, "To Boldly Go Where No [Man] Has Gone before"-Institutional Voids and the Development of Women's Digital Entrepreneurship," *Technological Forecasting and Social Change* (forthcoming). available: https://www.sciencedirect.com/science/article/pii/S0040162517317432

[19] D. Autor, D. Dorn, L. F. Katz, C. Patterson, and J. *Van* Reenen, *The Fall of the Labor Share and the Rise of Superstar Firms*, NBER (National Bureau of Economic Research), Cambridge, MA. (2017), available: https://www.nber.org/papers/w23396

[20] J. P. Allen, *Technology and Inequality: Concentrated Wealth in a Digital World*. Cham, Switzerland: Palgrave Macmillan, 2017.

[21] A. Martinez Dy, L. Martin, and S. Marlow, "Emancipation through Digital Entrepreneurship? A Critical Realist Analysis," *Organization*, vol. 25, no 5, pp. 585–608, 2018.

Choosing a Digital Business Idea

Highlights

Chapter 2 begins the process of choosing a digital business idea to prototype, and test.

- One of the first activities in digital entrepreneurship is choosing a digital business idea to prototype and test online.

- A good starting point for generating new ideas is to select from one of the most common types of digital business: content businesses, community businesses, online stores, and matchmaking businesses.

- Another common type of digital business promotes an already existing business in the 'real' world.

- Competitor research in the digital world is easier in some ways, but also more important with hundreds of millions of sites and apps competing for customer attention.

- Digital entrepreneurship offers many different revenue models to choose from, including advertisements, direct sales, subscriptions, donations, or the use of indirect revenue models such as generating sales leads.

Creativity and Innovation for Digital Entrepreneurs

A typical first step in digital entrepreneurship is choosing a new digital business idea to test. Finding a promising new business idea can be broken down into two separate but related processes: *creativity* and *innovation*. Creativity is the production of novel and useful ideas by an individual or small group. Innovation is the successful implementation of a new idea. While more creativity tends to lead to more innovation, there are often tensions between how novel an idea is and how practical it is to implement. While we might assume that smaller, more nimble startup businesses have an advantage when it comes to innovation, in traditional industries high creativity leads to successful innovation more often in larger firms with more resources [1]. Digital entrepreneurship might help change that picture.

There are many models of the creative process, but we will use a simple, classic model of creativity in organizations by Amabile [2] as a starting point. The creative process in this model has at least four stages: the initial *presentation* of a problem or opportunity, whether it is defined by others or comes from your own needs; *preparation*, or the previous knowledge you have of existing problems and solutions; idea *generation*; and idea *validation*, or the choice of which idea to pursue according to some criteria. Techniques for idea generation such as brainstorming or design workshops might be the first thing that come to mind when discussing creativity, but idea generation is only one stage of the creative process.

The effectiveness of the creative process in this model is influenced by at least three attributes of a person or group trying to perform a creative task: the *motivation* to do the task, whether it comes from within (*intrinsic* motivation) or is a requirement or incentive given by others (*extrinsic* motivation); the *skill level* in the area where innovation is taking place; and the person's or team's *creative thinking skills*.

Most studies find that intrinsic motivation leads to more creativity. When motivation comes from within, people tend to work harder. The intrinsically motivated are more likely to be resilient in the face of setbacks and are more confident about suggesting 'dumb' ideas that might be promising. If you are being required to learn digital entrepreneurship as part of a course at school or because it was suggested by someone else, it will be particularly useful for you to find some degree of intrinsic motivation to increase your creativity. As an individual, creativity can be increased by improving creative thinking skills such as practicing the ability to take on new and different perspectives and exposing yourself to different points of view [3].

While having a great new digital business idea to begin with is always helpful, don't let the lack of a perfect idea be a barrier to starting the journey. Digital technologies have increased the popularity of more 'feedback driven' approaches to finding great new ideas through experimentation [4] rather than solely relying on an early creative stage of idea generation. Learning how to be more creative is a useful skill, but the practical reality of digital entrepreneurship is that new business ideas usually evolve and change over time.

Common Types of Digital Businesses

As a beginning digital entrepreneur without a feel yet for what is possible, generating new business ideas is a challenge. One source of ideas is to follow what others do. In the digital world, popular new online businesses include: advertising-based content sites, blogs, e-commerce stores, graphics design services, and technical services [5]. In the offline world, the most popular areas for new businesses include: bed and breakfasts, beauty, catering and food, cleaning, consulting, skilled craftsperson services, gardening, home health care, home repair, music, personal assistants, personal trainers, pets, photography, property management, and sales [5]. Copying a business idea from one place and bringing it elsewhere where the idea hasn't been tried yet still counts as innovation. No one criticizes Starbuck's innovativeness just because they copied aspects of Italian coffee culture.

Another source of new business ideas is to consider trends. Trends might relate to particular types of people or life stages (demographics), new product and service possibilities, or simply new styles or fashions. A recent book argues that new parents, students, and older retirees are three promising demographics for new digital businesses [6]. Examples of popular product trends include sustainability, ethical sourcing, wellness and well-being, and homemade and handmade goods. Popular new style trends at this moment might include retro or hipster looks, but they are ever changing.

In our teaching, we've found that a useful starting point for generating new digital business ideas is to choose from one of the most common types of digital business. Each of these types addresses both the creativity and the innovation challenge—they are relatively straightforward to prototype but give the new entrepreneur lots of freedom to find a business that will be meaningful to them.

As a starting point, we offer five basic types of digital business. The first two types, content-based businesses and community-based businesses, focus on specialized areas of expertise or interest. The next two types, online stores and matchmaking, offer more traditional electronic commerce models based on sales or transaction fees. A fifth type, business promotion, attracts new customers to an already existing business.

Content-Based Business

A content-based business creates value by providing specialized content in digital form. The content can take many forms: articles, blog posts, images, memes, lists, FAQs, recipes and instructions, eBooks, directories, videos, and webinars to name a few. The list of potential topics is practically endless. Thanks to the global reach of the Internet and mobile devices, even the most seemingly obscure topic can find enough of a following to support the beginnings of a digital business.

Pure content businesses can be supported by a variety of revenue streams, but the ease of publishing online advertisements makes it an attractive default option. A core challenge of the content-based business, in addition to finding the right topic, is the work needed to keep content updated consistently.

Community-Based Business

A community-based business creates value by providing specialized content and conversations, which are contributed mostly by users. Just like a content-based business, the list of topics is almost endless, but the topic should be one where a community discussion makes the content more valuable. A vibrant community helps solve the content updating problem, but maintaining a community is hard work in itself. Communities can be more challenging to start, requiring more up-front effort and creativity to establish an initial critical mass of participants [7].

A community might generate revenue on its own, but can also support a variety of indirect activities that can increase business revenues or reduce business costs [8]. For example, on the revenue side, discussions in a digital community might be an important step in gathering information for a future purchase. For cost reduction, an online community might help with customer support or brand advocacy activities that a business would otherwise have to do themselves.

Online Store

An online store business sells products or services. The product might be physical or purely digital such as an e-book. The product can be something you make yourself or it could be sourced from a wholesaler or local producer. A great starting point for digital business is to team up with someone who has a product to sell but doesn't know how to create an online store to sell it. Another possibility is to sell your own expertise as a service if you have experience or credibility in a particular area.

The main revenue stream for an online store is straightforward—sales. A challenge for online stores that work with physical products is fulfillment and inventory. A real test of an online store idea requires actually creating a product or service and making it available for sale, even if it is only a minimal version at first. A whole universe of automated warehousing, order fulfillment, and shipping services has made testing an online store idea easier than ever, though the cost of these services can add up in the longer run. Once sales begin, digital entrepreneurs can use data to gain knowledge of customer preferences and find opportunities for cross-selling and upselling related products as well as potential subscription opportunities.

Matchmaking Business

A matchmaking business creates value by bringing together otherwise disconnected sets of people. A dating site is an obvious matchmaking business, but so would be a site that brings together students and tutors, or parents and babysitters, or hair stylists and people who need salon appointments [9]. So-called 'sharing economy' models blur the lines between producers and consumers by connecting ordinary people to share their physical goods or their own labor with others [10]. The digital world is able to bring together previous disconnected sets of people quickly and cheaply.

Matchmaking businesses are sometimes called two-sided markets in the sense that they connect two distinct user groups that are both required for the business to work. This can create a chicken-and-egg problem, where both groups need to be recruited and have enough participants to form a critical mass. If one group is more difficult to recruit, a common strategy is to make a matchmaking business cheaper or free to use for one group while charging the other group full price. A typical revenue stream would be transaction fees from successful matches or subscriptions.

Promotion Business

A promotion business is intended to attract new customers to a business that already exists, or will hopefully exist, in the real world. Millions of small businesses lack an effective (or any) online presence

[11], with a surprisingly high percentage suffering from basic problems such as incorrect contact information. Most existing businesses are interested in finding new customers, but customer acquisition in the digital world can be overwhelming for small business owners or startups.

One great strategy for starting in digital business is simply to find a small business that has a poor, missing, or ineffective online presence and make it your objective to attract new customers. A promotion business could attract visitors and have them contact a business, download information, sign up for a newsletter, or take advantage of a coupon or special deal. Digital promotion businesses can also be used to collect expressions of interest in an upcoming new business or product launch, though if the new business doesn't exist yet the value of obtaining a name and email address might be unclear.

Competitor Research

With billions of Internet users, there is never a shortage of potential customers online. But with hundreds of millions of web sites, social media profiles, and apps, there is never a shortage of potential competitors either. Assessing the competition for a new digital business idea is an important early step in the digital entrepreneurship process. A well-chosen competitor not only makes your own business idea clearer to others, it allows you to strengthen your idea by forcing you to clarify your *competitive advantage*: how your business will be either different or better.

Because of the size of the digital universe, defining potential competitors is not always straightforward.

Competitors can be identified by finding companies that target similar customer markets or by finding companies that use similar strategies and resources, or both [12]. Another way to identify competitors is by customer perceptions, or how consumers view the problems and solutions you are potentially offering [13]. There are also potentially indirect competitors, or companies who do not target the same market but instead offer a substitute product or service for similar customer needs.

No matter which technique is used, competitor research is more effective when the target customers for a new digital business idea are defined precisely. Many digital entrepreneurs create a persona, or brief sketch, of their target customer which includes both a biography and a statement of the goal they are trying to achieve [14]. The biography and the goal combine the two main aspects of customer identification: demographics and psychographics. By focusing on the goal to be achieved or the problem to be solved, the digital entrepreneur can pay more attention to the proposed benefits to the consumer or the customer value proposition rather than the technical features of the product.

The same channels used for customer acquisition—search and social media—can be the starting point for competitor research. For search, think about the phrases your target customers would use to achieve their goal (or ask them!). Do similar searches on the most relevant social media sites. Try to find social media profiles that are potential competitors for customer attention, but also could be role models for how to attract and engage a following in your space.

New digital business ideas can be too unfocused in the beginning. They might target too large an initial market, not appreciating the power of digital technology to make even the most highly specialized niche a potentially viable business. Attracting digital customers is often a winner-take-all game; consumers rarely look beyond the first page of search results or outside of their existing social networks. Dominating a niche, even a very small one, is often a better initial strategy than being merely okay in a larger market.

The end result of a quick online competitor search is sometimes a decision to change an idea or to focus even more intensely on a smaller niche. Once a new digital business is successful in its niche it will be better equipped to tackle larger markets as its search reputation and social media following grows.

Revenue Models

A thriving revenue stream is not always required in the experimental first phases of a new digital business, but trying to raise revenue is a powerful method for testing a proposed business idea. The digital world opens up a whole new set of potential revenue sources. Advertising and affiliate marketing allow any specialized content or conversation to be monetized. Transactions, subscriptions, and donations are all potential online revenue sources, but each with their own challenges, especially at the beginning. Digital entrepreneurs can also use the more traditional revenue model of selling a product or a service. Another option is to not raise revenue directly but instead focus on activities that will lead to revenue later. Generating customer leads is a prime example of this indirect revenue model.

There are few universal rules about which revenue models are best. Some factors may encourage a particular revenue model. An advertising revenue model works better with more users rather than less, all things being equal. Building a high amount of trust with customers makes payment models such as transactions more likely to succeed [15]. Table 2.1 contains preliminary suggestions for which revenue models may be more likely ('+') or less likely ('–') to work with different types of digital businesses, but these are suggestions based on experience rather than research results. Part of what makes digital entrepreneurship new is the ability to easily shift between different revenue models.

Advertising and Affiliate Marketing Revenue Models

The rise of advertisement publishing networks such as Google AdSense has made publishing advertisements on a web site as easy to use as cut and paste. Advertising networks can select from an inventory of millions of advertisements to find the ones most likely to generate revenue for your business. A digital business can earn revenue from displaying advertisements, but more revenue might come from the higher rates offered for

Table 2.1 Matching Revenue Models to Digital Business Types

	Content	Community	Store	Matchmaking	Promotion
Ads/Affiliate	+	+	–	+	–
Transactions		+	–	+	
Subscriptions			+		
Sales	+		+		
Donations		+	–		
Indirect	+	+	–		+

advertising clicks (the 'pay-per-click' model) rather than views, particularly for smaller businesses.

The advertising revenue model is convenient. It is a relatively easy way to monetize any content, but for advertisements to generate substantial revenue either the user base needs to grow or the content has to be well targeted at topics that advertisers are willing to pay higher amounts for, yet at the same time does not face excessive competition from other publishers. Some digital entrepreneurs worry that advertising revenue can be fragile, in the sense that it is not as sustainable as revenue models built on unique and durable assets such as customer lists, products, or experiences [16].

An affiliate marketing revenue model—also known as 'performance marketing'—is similar to an advertising model, but instead of being paid for advertisement clicks or displays, a publisher earns revenue only when a customer clicks through to another site and buys something. Each purchase earns a flat commission or a percentage of the sale. The largest affiliate marketing program in the US, Amazon Associates, starts their payments at around 4% of sales value with higher rates for more volume and special product campaigns. A digital business can sign up for a particular affiliate program or it can use an affiliate network to draw upon a larger inventory of advertisements.

In general, affiliate marketing revenue works better if content is directly related to a product purchase decision. An all-encompassing affiliate program like Amazon's makes it easy to find products for sale that match any digital content. Be careful not to be tempted by affiliate marketing programs with very high commissions for promoting questionable products.

Transaction Revenue Models

A transaction revenue model charges a flat fee or a percentage of total sales every time a transaction is successfully completed. Transactions work well with matchmaking businesses, because a successful match can create substantial value that a consumer is more willing to pay for than other kinds of online purchases. For example, consumers are very willing to pay 6–25% for a successful online room booking or 20–25% for a car sharing ride, not to mention 5–6% to buy or sell a house.

The transaction revenue model is more appropriate when consumers are accustomed to paying for services in your market. Because transaction fees may not be visible to the typical consumer, as when a traveler books a hotel room on a major travel site, your customers may be resistant to a separate transaction fee. Completing the transaction also needs to be convenient enough or provide enough additional value through guarantees or additional services that customers will not be tempted to finish transactions outside of your business.

Subscription Revenue Models

A subscription revenue model commits the consumer to regular, recurring payments. Product and service subscriptions are always popular with digital entrepreneurs because they offer a consistent, steady stream of revenue that has stickiness—consumers have to take action to stop sending you money. Subscriptions can work well for services delivered digitally, such as tutoring. Subscriptions to carefully chosen sets of products can be effective for consumers who enjoy discovery and variety. A common variant is a 'freemium' model, where a free level of service is offered to attract customers with the hope of upselling them to paid services with additional benefits.

One area where subscriptions have struggled is with content businesses. Unless the content is very unique or specialized there are likely to be many competing digital businesses offering free online content.

Sales Revenue Models

The classic revenue model of selling a product or service is easier than ever to implement online. Payment methods have become easy for digital entrepreneurs to sign up for, with transaction fees not much higher than traditional credit cards. For products and services that can be delivered digitally, such as an e-book, sales fulfillment is easy. Even for physical products there are many services available to make order fulfillment easier, or an entrepreneur can start by fulfilling orders on their own.

The main challenge of the sales revenue model is the amount of competition for online sales, both from specialized small businesses and from the giant platforms such as Amazon. The price competition for products that are available elsewhere can be quite intense, and dynamic pricing means entrepreneurs need a sophisticated strategy for monitoring price changes and responding to competitor moves [17].

A popular variant on sales revenue is the 'in-app purchase model'. For example, a mobile game could be downloaded and played for free but additional purchases in the game would add to a player's capability and enjoyment. This model is being tried in other contexts, such as paying to highlight comments in a community site or promote classified ads or news feed items. Like the 'freemium' model, only a small percentage of free users may convert to paid customers, requiring large numbers of users for the model to work.

Donation Revenue Models

Asking for donations has been a popular funding mechanism for small-scale digital projects, particularly when projects offer a community benefit such as free software. Donations are a tough sell for for-profit businesses unless they can be tied to some future consumer benefit, as with recent 'crowdfunding' models that offer early access to future products.

A great use of digital business is to raise money for a not-for-profit organization. A business could solicit donations directly or, if the target not-for-profit has its own online payment mechanism the digital business could forward potential donors to the not-for-profit. A digital business could experiment with new ways of attracting potential donors or new forms of engagement that will increase the likelihood of successful donations.

Customer Leads and Indirect Revenue Models

The revenue model for a digital business is *indirect* if the business does not generate revenue on its own, but instead creates actions that will lead to revenue elsewhere. A typical example of an indirect revenue model is generating new customer leads. The more complicated a sales process, the less likely that a visitor will arrive at a site and buy immediately. As an example, the sales process for a consulting firm might have multiple steps where a potential customer first seeks out background information, client testimonials, and maybe a personal discussion or consultation before agreeing to become a client. For these complex sales processes, particularly in a business-to-business (B2B) context rather than consumer sales (B2C), a successful digital business finds customers and moves them through the sales process rather than makes sales directly.

An indirect model is well suited for a promotion business where seeking new customers is the main objective. A challenge for indirect revenue models is the problem of testing a new digital business idea. If the indirect activity is closely connected to a sale, such as a request for a consultation or an appointment, then it is easier to tell if a digital business idea is effective. If the indirect activity is too far removed from a sales transaction it can be difficult to know whether activities such as information downloads or content shares truly lead to revenue. The more data there is on the entire sales process, the more effective an indirect model can be.

No matter which digital business type is chosen, and which revenue model, the more important issue is to get started. The next step will be to create a digital business design, a single page statement of how your proposed digital business will work.

Additional Resources

www.google.com/adsense/start/ — Google AdSense, a large advertising network friendly to beginning publishers.
www.associateprograms.com/directory — directory of affiliate marketing programs.
https://mthink.com/best-cps-affiliate-networks/ — another directory of affiliate marketing programs.
www.ecommercetimes.com/ — news about e-commerce topics and different revenue models.

Exercises

2.1. Discuss how you will find the intrinsic motivation (motivation from within) to pursue a digital entrepreneurship project.

2.2. Describe a promising trend that could create a new digital business opportunity.

2.3. Use one of the five common types of digital business to create a new digital business idea focused on an opportunity that you have a personal interest in or expertise about.

2.4. Use one of the five common types of digital business to create a new digital business idea focused on an opportunity that you have little or no experience with.

2.5. Find a small business whose online presence is either missing or is less effective than it could be. Propose a new digital business idea that will create value for this small business.

2.6. List the three most important competitors for a proposed digital business idea. Describe your proposed competitive advantage over each of these competitors.

2.7. Choose two different potential revenue models for a proposed digital business idea. For each model evaluate how much revenue might be raised from the first 1000 customers.

References

[1] H. Sarooghi, D. Libaers, and A. Burkemper, "Examining the Relationship Between Creativity and Innovation: A Meta-Analysis of Organizational, Cultural, and

Environmental Factors," *Journal of Business Venturing*, vol. 30, no. 5, pp. 714–731, 2015.

[2]   T. M. Amabile, "A Model of *Creativity* and Innovation in Organizations," *Research in Organizational Behavior*, vol. 10, no. 1, pp. 123–167, 1988.

[3]   C. E. Shalley and L. L. Gilson, "What Leaders Need to Know: A Review of Social and Contextual Factors That Can Foster or Hinder Creativity," *The Leadership Quarterly*, vol. 15, no. 1, pp. 33–53, 2004.

[4]   B. Feld and S. Wise, *Startup Opportunities: Know When to Quit Your Day Job*. Hoboken, NJ: John Wiley & Sons, 2017.

[5]   R. Stim and L. Guerin, *Running a Side Business: How to Create a Second Income*. Berkeley, CA: Nolo, 2009.

[6]   B. Schwerdt, *How to Build an Online Business*. Hoboken, NJ: John Wiley & Sons, 2018.

[7]   C. Young, "Community Management That Works: How to Build and Sustain a Thriving Online Health Community," *Journal of Medical Internet Research*, vol. 15, no. 6, 2013.

[8]   D. Ryan, *Understanding Digital Marketing: Marketing Strategies for Engaging the Digital Generation*. London: Kogan Page Publishers, 2016.

[9]   C. O'Connor. *Styleseat Ceo on Raising $40m for Beauty Booking Startup Despite Biased Vcs*. (2016), available: www.forbes.com/sites/clareoconnor/2016/07/26/ styleseat-ceo-on-raising-40m-for-beauty-booking- startup-despite-biased-vcs/. [Accessed: September 3, 2018].

[10]   C. Richter, S. Kraus, A. Brem, S. Durst, and C. Giselbrecht, "Digital Entrepreneurship: Innovative Business Models for the Sharing Economy," *Creativity and Innovation Management*, vol. 26, no. 3, pp. 300– 310, 2017.

[11]   A. Peacock. *Small Business Websites in 2017: Survey*. (2017), available: https://clutch.co/web-designers/ resources/small-business-2017-website-survey. [Accessed: June 6, 2018].

[12]   M. J. Chen, "Competitor Analysis and Interfirm Rivalry: Toward a Theoretical Integration," *Academy of Management Review*, vol. 21, no. 1, pp. 100–134, 1996.

[13] F. A. Gur and T. Greckhamer, "Know Thy Enemy: A Review and Agenda for Research on Competitor Identification," *Journal of Management*, doi: 10.1177/0149206317744250, 2018.

[14] D. Croxen-John and J. van Tonder, *E-Commerce Website Optimization: Why 95 Per Cent of Your Webiste Visitors Don't Buy and What You Can Do About It.* London: Kogan Page, 2017.

[15] A. Enders, H. Hungenberg, H.-P. Denker, and S. Mauch, "The Long Tail of Social Networking: Revenue Models of Social Networking Sites," *European Management Journal*, vol. 26, no. 3, pp. 199–211, 2008.

[16] P. Marshall, K. Krance, and T. Meloche, *Ultimate Guide to Facebook Advertising: How to Access 1 Billion Potential Customers in 10 Minutes*, 2nd ed. Irvine, CA: Entrepreneur Press, 2015.

[17] L. Chen, A. Mislove, and C. Wilson, An Empirical Analysis of Algorithmic Pricing on Amazon Marketplace," in *Proceedings of the 25th International Conference on World Wide Web*, 2016, pp. 1339–1349: International World Wide Web Conferences Steering Committee.

Creating a Digital Business Design

Highlights

Chapter 3 shows how to create a digital business design—a high level overview of the main aspects of a digital business that can be captured in a short document.

- A digital business design starts with a value proposition, describing the purpose of a digital business and its competitive advantage versus alternatives.

- The core digital business process is described as a simple three step 'ABC' process: Acquisition, Behavior, and Conversion.

- The first step is customer *acquisition*: how many potential customers will you attract online, and where will they come from?

- The second step is visitor *behavior*: what will potential customers do or see at a digital business that will make them want to become customers?

- The third step is the *conversion*: what specific action will potential customers take that represents business success, such as a purchase, an advertisement click, or a contact request? What percentage of online visitors will successfully 'convert'?

- The conversion equation is a statement of how many visits will lead to successful conversions. The conversion equation can be thought of as a hypothesis, or informed guess, about a proposed digital business that will be tested by a prototype.

The ABCs of Digital Business Design: The Acquisition-Behavior-Conversion Process

A digital business design is a high-level overview of the main aspects of a digital business. The design is a simplified model that can help transform a business idea into a specific test that can be implemented through a prototype.

A digital business design begins with a value proposition describing the purpose of a digital business and its competitive advantage with respect to competitors. The previous chapter discussed how to generate ideas for the overall purpose of a new digital business using one of five basic types, and how to find competitors. The overall purpose and competitive positioning provide a value proposition for customers, but also a clear reason for the entrepreneur and any potential partners or investors to participate as well.

A digital business design is structured around a simple three-step process, or the ABCs: Acquisition, Behavior, and Conversion. The initial test of a digital business idea will be to try to acquire or attract new visitors, invite visitors to do something online, and then convert a visitor into a customer by having them perform an action that has value for a business. The ABCs are inspired by the world of web analytics, which organizes much of its data around these three key activities.

Two things to note about the ABC process. First, a digital entrepreneur needs to optimize the entire process, not just a particular step. It is easy to acquire visitors by promising something (free donut! Click here), but a visitor will only convert if the experience is positive, and the promise is fulfilled. Second, a digital business design is a more appropriate model for the early testing phases. There is much more to consider about customer retention and overall lifetime customer value, for example, than just the initial acquisition process [1], and user experience is a more complex issue than simply online behavior. But the ABC process is a useful starting point for testing.

Acquisition: Finding Customers Online

The first step in the ABC process is acquiring customers online. A digital business design specifies how many visitors are being targeted and which sources, or channels, they will arrive from. Digital marketing offers a variety of techniques that are 'designed to drive targeted, pre-qualified traffic to your website' [2]. For a typical digital business, two of the most frequently used sources of customers are search results and social media platforms. The task for the digital entrepreneur will be to entice users to click on links at search and social media sites and visit your digital business.

Search results have become one of the most important tools for consumer decision making. In the US, one survey found that 71% of consumers use search to find new products and services, and 74% use search to decide what to buy [3]. Consumers also have high trust in the quality of search results, viewing them as only slightly less trustworthy than recommendations from people they know, and more trustworthy than almost any other source of information.

Most people looking for information only see the top few search results, even though entering a typical phrase into a search engine might return millions of web pages. Being the top search result will likely attract the most visitors, with an average of 25–35% of searchers clicking on a result and continuing on to your online business. This click-through rate drops off rapidly as a digital business moves further down the results page. If a digital business sinks below the first page of top ten results, the percentage of searchers who will click through and visit a business drops to an average of 1% and below [4].

Because being a top search result is so important for customer acquisition, and with so much competition for those top results, it is vital for a digital business to carefully target the search phrases that customers will use to find them. As a starting point, a digital business design chooses the most important phrase to target first. A good initial search phrase will be meaningful for potential customers and attract enough traffic to meet the needs of a digital business test, yet not have too much high quality competition from other web pages for search results.

Social media has become hugely important for customer acquisition because of the amount of time people spend on social networks and the importance of personal recommendations, product reviews, and other forms of 'electronic word of mouth' in purchasing decisions. Consumers find out about new products on two different kinds of social media—social networks and dedicated product review sites—but tend to use review sites more when deciding which product or service to purchase [3].

A digital business design includes the most important social media platform where customer acquisition efforts will be concentrated at first. While the dominant personal social network (for example, Facebook in the US) might seem an obvious choice, don't forget product review communities, social media focused on content types such as images or video, and social media platforms targeted at specific groups or uses such as LinkedIn for professional use.

As a first take on social media strategy, the design will briefly describe the content that will be provided on social media to stimulate customer interest, the frequency of updating, and the number of followers needed to generate visitor traffic. Regularly updated content is important for keeping a social media presence effective, so a digital business needs to know where this content will come from and how frequently it needs to be updated. For example, product review sites don't require daily updates but depend on a critical mass of content, while a microblogging site like Twitter is more effective with multiple updates per day.

On personal social networking sites, potential customers are much more likely to see your content if they are a follower or subscriber. A major part of social media strategy is building a following. For the digital business design, estimate the number of social media followers that will generate sufficient visitor traffic. Think about how often the content seen by followers will attract users to click through to a digital business.

Behavior: What Customers Do Online

The second step in the ABC process is visitor behavior. What will potential customers do or see at a digital business that will make them want to become customers? Visitors arrive at a digital business in response to a need or desire to do something. The potential customer might intend to make a purchase at a certain price, gather information, make a comment, or just be entertained. The digital world provides information and tools for the rational side of our brains, but it is also a place of creativity and self-expression [5]. There is plenty of room for digital entrepreneurs to find creative new ways of serving unfulfilled customer needs, both rational and emotional.

Of course, for visitor behavior to happen, the visitor must have an online presence to visit. The starting point for an online presence is usually a website, located at a specific domain name. The domain name (such as google.com, or usfca.edu) is the address used to find a digital business on the Internet, but a domain name is also part of a brand that signals to a visitor that a business is relevant and trustworthy. Choosing a domain name that sends the right message to potential customers, but isn't already taken, can be a challenge.

To satisfy the most important customer need, a digital business design includes the most important use case. A use case is a task that a user will perform on a website, beginning with a user goal, and ending when that goal is fulfilled [6]. If a customer is trying to purchase a specific product, for example, the most important use case will include finding that product and entering in the information for a transaction. If a customer is looking for specific content, the use case will include finding that content. A potential customer should be able to successfully complete the most important use case without difficulty and be satisfied in a way that leads to a successful business outcome.

Conversion: The Definition of Success

Digital entrepreneurship benefits greatly from the ability to measure and track business success at a detailed level. The third step in the ABC process is conversion, or the specific action a visitor will perform online that represents business success. Examples of successful conversions include buying a product or service, contacting a business for an appointment or consultation, or clicking on an advertisement and being taken to another site. The appropriate conversion will depend on the type of digital business and its business objective.

Instead of thinking of a website as a beautiful brochure or as a source of content, think of a digital business site as a 'conversion engine'. 'It is your website that converts that traffic into prospects and customers . . . transforming them into something valuable for your business' [2]. The primary focus of technology building efforts should be creating conversions.

In the early years of digital marketing, online channels were criticized for being less effective at conversions than channels involving personal contact [1]. Today customer expectations have changed, and constant experimentation can increase digital conversion rates over time. What remains true is that lengthier interactions, perhaps over multiple visits, make visitors more likely to convert on average. There are often synergies, or positive relationships, between digital channels and other traditional forms of contact.

Conversion goals for a digital business are the specific, measurable digital actions that reflect a conversion. Examples include a 'buy now' button click, an advertisement click, or a 'submit contact form' button click. By tracking conversion goals through web analytics, digital entrepreneurs have a clear way of measuring the success of their tests. By making changes to their digital business and seeing whether conversion goals increase or decrease, the digital entrepreneur can optimize and improve their business ideas.

The Conversion Equation: A Digital Business Hypothesis

A conversion equation for a digital business is a quick summary of how the business is expected to perform. The conversion equation multiplies the desired number of visitors in a time period (usually per month) times a conversion rate to calculate the number of conversions a business is trying to achieve. The conversion rate is the percentage of visitors that fulfill a conversion goal.

The conversion rate is a measure of the effectiveness of the overall ABC process. At the beginning, conversion rates are likely to be low. Between 1–10% might be a good initial estimate, depending on how demanding the conversion goal is—sales and transactions ask more of visitors than newsletter signups or downloads.

Conversion rates in a mature digital business are often below 5%, which is perfectly acceptable because of the high visitor numbers that digital businesses can attract.

For the first test of a digital business idea, only a few real conversions are needed. Too few, and testing might take too long to give results. Too many conversions might be unrealistic before visitor numbers can be built up. From the conversion rate estimate and the number of conversions required, the digital entrepreneur can calculate the number of visitors required for the initial test. The visitor number in the conversion equation can then be used to check whether the initial customer acquisition estimates are sufficient.

The conversion equation is a kind of hypothesis, or educated guess, about the strength of a digital business idea. The equation is more a tool for surfacing assumptions and providing a clear goal for experiments than it is about predicting the right answer. Once a digital business begins, an important goal will be to increase, or optimize, the conversion rate through experimentation [7]. There are general guidelines for increasing conversion rates, such as design changes that make customer value more obvious or endorsements that build customer trust, but for the creative entrepreneur the digital world makes it possible to try out and evaluate many different ideas for how to improve the business.

The Digital Business Design

A single page format for a digital business design is included in the appendix. Here are some tips and reminders for what to fill in each box:

Business Goals and Objectives

Type of digital business: start with one of the five basic types of digital business: content-based, community-based, online store, matchmaking, or promotion.

Business objective: describe what your digital business is trying to achieve in one sentence. For example, "be the best online source for information about pet lizard care". Or, "increase the number of new customers at a local coffee shop". Or, "match local dog walkers in San Francisco with students who would like to walk them". Another possibility is to state the type of online business, along with its specialization, for example:

- A content business about [*fill in the topic*].

- A community business about [*fill in the topic*].

- An online store selling [*fill in the products or services*].

- A matchmaking business connecting [*fill in group A*] [and *fill in group B if there's a second group*].

- A business promoting [*fill in existing real-world business*].

Competitors

Closest competitor: give the web address (URL) for the online competitor that comes the closest to the target customer, product or service, or strategy of the proposed digital business.

How will you be different or better? In one short sentence, describe what you think your competitive advantage will be over this competitor. Either you will do something differently or you will do the same thing but better. How?

Acquisition

Keyword search phrase: give the exact phrase that
you believe will lead to the target number of visitors
coming to your digital business and then successfully
converting. If the phrase has too much strong
competition, your digital business is unlikely to show
up near the top of the search results and won't
generate any visitor traffic.

Visitors/month: estimate how many visitors per month
will arrive at your digital business based on search
results from your chosen phrase. If you can, sign up
for a service such as Google AdWords that provides
data on how many people search that phrase in a
given month. If not enough people are searching
on the chosen phrase, the visitors per month target
cannot be met without investing in some kind of
advertising or promotion campaign. A phrase with
zero searches is obviously not a good target for
customer acquisition.

Behavior

Available domain name: list a domain name that is
appropriate for the business but is also available and
unregistered by someone else. A domain name that
is available for sale at a price higher than a standard
registration fee (anywhere from $1–40 USD per
year, depending on the top-level domain at the end)
is already owned by someone else. Once a test is
successful, then a business can consider buying a
more expensive domain name.

Most important use case: in one sentence, describe a
task that a visitor will expect to perform at your digital
business and that will fulfill a visitor's goal. Successful

completion of this task should meet customer expectations and encourage them to successfully convert.

Conversions

Primary conversion goal: list the specific digital action a visitor will perform that reflects business success. Examples include clicking on a 'buy now' button, clicking to submit a contact form, clicking on an advertisement, or clicking to subscribe to a newsletter.

Revenue stream: choose one of the most common revenue streams for digital businesses, including advertising or affiliate marketing, transaction fees, subscriptions, sales, or donations. If there is no direct revenue stream, write 'indirect' and briefly state the value that the customer leads or other actions will have for your business. Earning revenue in the early stages is not as important as using revenue as a test of the quality of a new business idea.

Conversion Equation

Visitors/month: how many visitors per month expected from customer acquisition activities. The number of visitors should be comparable to the visitors expected from the preceding search and social media channels.

% conversion rate: give the initial conversion rate estimate, most likely below 10%. This rate will be adjusted up or down later when there is real data to compare with.

Conversions/month: multiply the visitors/month by the conversion rate to obtain this number. The number of conversions should be sufficient to test your digital business idea in the time you have available.

Alternatives to a Digital Business Design

The one-page digital business design is specifically intended to test an early digital prototype. It is helpful because it provides a performance target and prioritizes the implementation activities in all three critical areas: acquisition, behavior, and conversion. There are alternative methods for providing an overview of what is sometimes called the 'business model' of a proposed business idea. Two popular alternatives are the Business Model Canvas by Osterwalder and Pigneur [8], and the framework from *Disciplined Entrepreneurship* by Aulet [9].

The Business Model Canvas gives a more complete overview of a proposed business, but still fits on a single page. It consists of four main parts. First, the customer value proposition, or how the business will solve customer problems and serve their needs. Second, how value will be provided or delivered to the customer, by specifying the exact customer segments to be targeted, what relationships will be built with customers, and which channels will be used to communicate with them and deliver services. Third, the assets required to deliver customer value, including key resources, key activities, and key partnerships. Fourth, the proposed cost structure and revenue streams that will support the business. The digital business design used in this book is a simplification of the full Business Model Canvas that assumes assets, customers, and revenue are all located in the digital world.

Another alternative is the framework from *Disciplined Entrepreneurship*, which is intended to describe a high-growth, high-technology startup. The framework asks for detailed answers to these six questions:

- Who is your customer?

- What can you do for your customer?

- How does your customer acquire your product?

- How do you make money from your product?

- How do you design and build your product?

- How do you scale your business?

Whether you use the one-page digital business design, one of these other design methods, or some combination, the important outcome at this early stage of digital entrepreneurship is to clarify the assumptions behind an idea for a new digital business. Digital entrepreneurs usually have a much clearer idea of the customer problem they want to solve than the exact details of the 'business model' that will solve it in a practical and sustainable way—they 'fake it until they make it' [10].

The design is your informed guess, or hypothesis, about a digital business. If a prototype is built with this conversion goal, user behavior, and customer acquisition strategy the design predicts the number of conversions that can be expected. The next step will be to create a prototype, get your idea in the hands of potential customers as quickly as possible, and start learning.

Additional Resources

The one-page Digital Business Design in the Appendix.

Exercises

3.1. Fill in a one-page digital business design for a proposed new business idea. Get feedback on your design from at least two other people and comment on their feedback.

3.2. For your keyword search phrase find the number of searches performed on that phrase per month. Are there enough searches to satisfy your customer acquisition goals?

3.3. Describe why you think the user experience of your digital business, in particular your most important use case, will make potential customers want to convert.

References

[1]   W. Reinartz, J. S. Thomas, and V. Kumar, "Balancing Acquisition and Retention Resources to Maximize Customer Profitability," *Journal of Marketing*, vol. 69, no. 1, pp. 63–79, 2005.

[2]   D. Ryan, *Understanding Digital Marketing: Marketing Strategies for Engaging the Digital Generation*. London: Kogan Page Publishers, 2016.

[3]   Forrester Research. *Why Search + Social = Success for Brands: The Role of Search and Social in the Customer Life Cycle*. 2016, available: www.catalystdigital.com/wp-content/uploads/WhySearchPlusSocialEqualsSuccess-Catalyst.pdf.

[4]   Advanced Web Ranking. *Google Organic Ctr History*. (2018), available: www.advancedwebranking.com/cloud/ctrstudy/. [Accessed: June 15, 2018].

[5]   C. Lamberton and A. T. Stephen, "A Thematic Exploration of Digital, Social Media, and Mobile Marketing: Research Evolution from 2000 to 2015 and

an Agenda for Future Inquiry," *Journal of Marketing*, vol. 80, no. 6, pp. 146–172, 2016.

[6]   Usability.gov. *Use Cases*. (2018), available: www.usability.gov/how-to-and-tools/methods/use-cases.html. [Accessed: September 2, 2018].

[7]   D. Croxen-John and J. van Tonder, *E-Commerce Website Optimization: Why 95 Per Cent of Your Webiste Visitors Don't Buy and What You Can Do About It*. London: Kogan Page, 2017.

[8]   A. Osterwalder and Y. Pigneur, *Business Model Generation: A Handbook for Visionaries, Game Changers, and Challengers*. Hoboken, NJ: John Wiley & Sons, 2010.

[9]   B. Aulet, *Disciplined Entrepreneurship: 24 Steps to a Successful Startup*. Hoboken, NJ: John Wiley & Sons, 2013.

[10]   C. Standing and J. Mattsson, ""Fake It until You Make It": Business Model Conceptualization in Digital Entrepreneurship," *Journal of Strategic Marketing*, vol. 26, no. 5, pp. 385–399, 2018.

Building a Business Prototype

Highlights

Chapter 4 begins the process of creating a web prototype for a digital business, using freely available software and inexpensive Internet technology.

- A web site prototype can be used to implement and test a digital business design.

- Entrepreneurs building a prototype need to acquire a domain name that is available and effective for successfully converting customers.

- Inexpensive and powerful web hosting services make it easy to publish simple web pages and create more sophisticated software-based sites that can be used for real business applications.

- Content management software is a good multipurpose tool for creating digital business prototypes. The majority of web sites use content management software to organize and deliver their online presence to customers.

- By the end of this chapter, the reader should be able to create simple web pages and (for now, empty) prototype sites and make them available through the Internet via their own domain name.

Using Prototypes to Test a Digital Business Design

Building a prototype for a business idea and trying it out is where the advantages of digital entrepreneurship really begin to shine. A prototype acts as a Minimum Viable Product (MVP), giving entrepreneurs a tool to start experimenting with their business and to learn quickly. An MVP is deliberately kept simple to get it in the hands of customers quickly, but also to make learning more effective by testing only the most important assumptions about a new business idea at any given time.

An MVP for a business in the non-digital world can be as simple as a flyer, a table at a local farmer's market, or a workshop at a local community center. An MVP in the digital world has the advantages of being easy to create, easy to edit, and easy to deliver. A digital MVP could be as basic as a piece of content like a video, podcast, webinar, or white paper [1]. But the default choice for a digital MVP is normally a web site. A web site with a domain name is the simplest business asset an entrepreneur can own, control, and build a following for without being subject to another company's ever-changing terms of service.

How difficult is it to build a prototype web site? Quite easy these days. With a domain name and a web hosting service, an entrepreneur can make a surprisingly powerful web site available to billions of people around the world. Web pages can be coded by hand, but a web site today is more likely to be created and managed by specialized software. Web hosting services make it easy to launch sophisticated, software-backed sites that can be used for real business applications.

In this chapter, we present the basics of digital business prototyping: domain names, web hosting, web pages, style sheets, and content management software. By the end of this chapter the reader should be able to create simple web pages and (for now, empty) prototype sites that are available through the Internet at your own domain name.

Prototype Building Options

The main options for creating an online presence include:

- Using a profile on an existing platform (such as a Facebook profile or Instagram account).

- Using a web page or site builder offered by another company.

- Using freely available software to create and manage a web site on your own server using your own domain name.

- Custom coding a web site.

- Custom coding a mobile app.

Using a social media platform such as a Facebook profile for prototyping has the advantage of requiring near-zero technical knowledge, little or no cost, and large potential audience of followers for content. The main disadvantages are the lack of control and lack of ownership. Any business activity on another company's platform is subject to their approval. One wrong post or image and an entrepreneur could be shut out of their own business. The terms of service for the large platforms typically restrict how an account can be used as a business asset, for example by restricting the ability to transfer or sell an account or to access your own list of customers.

Online business and electronic commerce experts recommend building the brand reputation of a web site and a domain name in most situations [2]. Schwerdt says to 'treat your website as the mothership' because from a business perspective, 'your website is an asset you own' [1]. Other platforms can then act as traffic sources that send visitors to an entrepreneur's most valuable online property: their web site and domain. A platform account can make sense if it offers specialized capabilities such as an online store or shopping cart.

Choosing to build a prototype with a web site requires at least two things: a domain name that provides the address of the prototype, or where to find it; and a web hosting service that will store a web site on a server connected to the Internet and make it available to anyone who asks. A web hosting service can be used to make custom-coded web pages available online, but for business prototyping it is often easier to use web sites that are created and managed by software. For a web site that has to be very fast or unique, custom coding a web site has advantages [3]. Creating and managing a site with software, however, allows prototyping to be started without coding.

A web site driven by software will typically offer a regular version of the site and a version optimized for mobile use. A mobile-optimized web site is often a good enough starting point for mobile prototyping. The alternative is to custom code a mobile app either for Apple iOS or Google Android or both, requiring some programming skills. The pros and cons of mobile app development are discussed in Chapter 13.

For the majority of digital business prototyping by non-expert coders, a web site driven by software is a good general purpose tool that is not too difficult but can be adapted to fit the business as it evolves. The following sections discuss what is needed to get started. The 'Road to the Prototype' document in the Appendix offers a step-by-step set of technical activities that lead to a prototype web site available on the Internet.

Web Sites and Domain Name Basics

A digital business prototype can be implemented with a web site available on the Internet at a specific domain name. How does this all work? Understanding what's going on behind the scenes means knowing a little bit about how the Internet works, how domain names work, and what web pages are.

First, the Internet, everyone's favorite global network. The story of how this grassroots, peer-to-peer network took over the world is a truly miraculous one. For the digital entrepreneur, the key to understanding the Internet is simply to know that it does one job: move digital information from one computer on the network to another.

The information being transferred can be anything that exists in a digital format: a document, a picture, a song, or a database with a list of customers. The digital information being sent over the Internet might also be a request for one computer to do something for the other (the machine asking for something is the *client*, while the machine fulfilling the request is the *server*). Special digital languages called *protocols* define what can be asked for, and how. For example, computers on the Internet can use an email protocol (SMTP is one) to ask for any new messages at a particular mailing address, or a file sharing protocol (FTP) to request a specific file.

For a computer to send and receive digital information on the Internet, it needs to be connected to the Internet and have a unique Internet address so that other machines can find it. Connections to the Internet are offered by specialized companies, including Internet service providers, cloud services providers, and web hosts. Internet addresses are in the form of IP addresses. For example, as of this writing, 172.217.15.110 is the IP address of a server that handles requests for the google. com web site.

Because numbers like 172.217.15.110 are not the easiest for people to deal with, the Internet also includes a Domain Naming System (DNS) that allows the use of domain names, such as google.com, to find things. A domain name registrar is a company that rents out domain names not already being used, usually by the year, and keeps track of records such as the IP address associated with a domain name. In most but not all top-level domains (TLDs)—the part of the domain name after the dot, such as. com—domain name registrations can be bought and sold freely.

Most geeks prefer to interact with digital technology through a command line interface (i.e., the Terminal utility on Apple machines, or the Command Prompt on Windows machines). Command line interfaces are incredibly powerful once you master their arcane commands. However, normal humans prefer a friendly graphical interface such as the world wide web, or web for short. The web consists of three standards that work together to make human-friendly web pages accessible via the Internet:

- A special language for describing the content of web pages, called HTML (HyperText Markup Language).

- A protocol for requesting web pages, called HTTP (HyperText Transport Protocol).

- A standard for specifying the unique address of each web page, usually called a URL (Uniform Resource Locator).

A web page is a plain text document written in HTML that can be displayed in a friendly graphical form by web browser software. HTML consists of tags, usually in pairs, which categorize content on a web page such as a pair of tags for each paragraph, or a pair of tags for the title of a page. A URL for a web page, such as www.usfca.edu/management/faculty/jonathan-allen consists of a domain name (usfca.edu) where the document can be found, the exact name and location of the document (i.e., a document called 'jonathan-allen', within a directory called 'faculty', within a directory called 'management'), and the method used to request the document (i.e., HTTPS, a newer version of HTTP that is more secure).

To summarize, this is what a digital business prototype consists of: a web site, made up of one or more web pages that can be found at a domain name registered to you. Each web page has its own URL. By typing the right URL into a web browser address bar or by clicking on a link or image that points to the right URL, a visitor is brought to your digital business prototype site. The domain name of a requested web page is translated by the DNS into the IP address of the server computer that has access to the document. With the correct IP address the Internet can then do its magic and send information back and forth from the web browser software on the client device to the web server software on the server machine. People connected to the Internet can now interact with your digital business from almost any device, anytime, anywhere.

Choosing a Domain Name

A web site prototype requires a domain name, preferably one that is unique to your business. A relevant, meaningful domain name adds to the effectiveness of any digital business prototype. The first step is to find a domain name available for purchase. Specialized companies called domain name registrars allow entrepreneurs to search for available domains and purchase them. Some of the largest registrars include godaddy.com (US), tucows. com (Canada), and 1and1.com (Germany).

An early decision will be which Top Level Domain (TLD) to choose from. Over 70% of domain registrations are in the .com TLD. Because .com domain names are so popular, they are the best known and tend to convey more trust to visitors. Domain names ending in .net are about 7% of registrations, and .org about 6%. Good .com domain names that are still available can be difficult to find. When deciding between a better domain name ending in .net and a less desirable domain name ending in .com, consider the additional trust a potential customer might place in a relatively unknown .com name and the difficulty of trying to compete against the .com version of your own name. Recently over a thousand new Top Level Domains were created, including .bar, .club, .eco, .top, and even .sucks. Because these TLDs are so new, it's hard to predict how well they will perform compared to the familiar .com.

Within the domain names themselves try to avoid hyphens, numbers, and deliberate misspellings that will be difficult for potential customers to remember. An unknown name with a strange spelling will require that much more investment in brand awareness, resources that could be spent on improving the product instead. Regardless of the name chosen, not having your own domain name comes across as unprofessional to potential customers [2].

Once a domain name is found a digital entrepreneur can purchase the domain name in one of two ways. First, a domain name can be purchased at a domain name registrar. The domain name can be bought first and the registrar company can be told later where the prototype web site will be hosted on the Internet. Second, the domain name can be purchased later at a web hosting company. Web hosting services are needed to make your web site available over the Internet, and these services often include domain name registration as part of the price of their web hosting packages.

Choosing a Web Hosting Service

Digital entrepreneurs need to find a home for their prototype web sites. A cheap and relatively simple solution is to use a web hosting service. The web host makes files, documents, and web pages available through the Internet and allows the installation of software to create and manage more sophisticated web sites.

Most low-cost web hosting services offer similar capabilities in terms of file storage space and networking capacity. The most important capability for prototyping is the ability to install specialized web site software such as WordPress, the world's most popular content management software. Another useful feature is the ability to use multiple domain names and install multiple web sites within a single account. Most additional features offered for sale can be added on later, though customers are increasingly expecting web sites to use the more secure HTTPS protocol, which requires a special authentication key called an SSL certificate. Quality customer service and support are worth spending a little bit more for, in case something goes wrong at an inconvenient time during your class or your professional life.

The cheapest level of web hosting is called shared hosting because web pages and files are sharing a server with many other accounts. The processing power of shared hosting isn't the greatest, but it should be good enough for your first few thousand visitors per month. Another option for web hosting is to use a cloud services provider such as Amazon Web Services. Cloud services are becoming easier to use for non-experts, but as of this writing still require some command line expertise. This option is discussed in Chapter 13.

Setting Up Web Hosting

Web hosting accounts make web pages, files, and documents available on the Internet. Anyone connected to the Internet with a web browser should be able to type in the correct URL using your domain name and see the correct web page, file, or document. For example, by entering http://jpedia.org/jpchicken.jpeg in the address bar of a web browser, you should see the image file called 'jpchicken.jpeg' that has been uploaded to the web hosting account of the jpedia.org domain.

The domain name needs to be directed to a web hosting account for this to work properly. If the domain name was registered through the web hosting company at the same time web hosting was purchased then the domain name should already be directed to your web hosting account. You can test this by typing your domain name into a web browser address bar. You should see a generic web page from your web hosting service, not an error message.

If the domain name was purchased at a separate domain name registrar, then there are two steps to connecting the domain name to a web hosting account. First, sign into the account at the domain name registrar and change the nameservers for your domain name to point to your web hosting service. For example, an account at the web host bluehost.com uses the nameserver addresses ns1.bluehost.com and ns2.bluehost.com. Other web hosts will have their own nameserver addresses.

The second step is to add your domain name to your web hosting account if it was not already added in the web hosting signup process. Each web host has its own procedure for adding domain names, but be sure to add the domain rather than transfer ownership. Transferring domain name ownership is a lengthy process, and not necessary if the nameservers are already directed to the web host. It may take a few hours for a nameserver change to work its way through the Internet DNS. If successful, typing your domain name into a browser should show a generic web page from your web hosting service and not your domain name registrar.

Uploading Files to a Web Host

The web hosting service stores files and documents using directories (or folders) in the same way as personal computers. After logging on to your web hosting account, there should be a 'file manager' or similar option for viewing the directories and files at your account.

One of these directories will be designated as the public web directory. The name of this special directory is 'public_html' for bluehost.com accounts but might be different at other web hosts. Every file inside this directory is available throughout the Internet via your domain name. For example, the file 'jpchicken.jpeg' is inside the 'public_html' directory of the jpedia.org web hosting account. The entire Internet can view this image at jpedia.org/jpchicken.jpeg.

Try using the 'file manager' at your web hosting account to upload a few images or documents to your public web directory. Test your work by opening a web browser and typing your domain name, followed by a forward slash '/', followed by the complete and exact name of an uploaded file. Your file should appear not only in your own web browser, but in anyone else's connected to the Internet.

Uploading and downloading files to the web hosting account is easier if you use special software called an FTP client on your personal computer. Popular FTP clients include Filezilla and Cyberduck. If you wish to use an FTP client, download the software to your personal computer first. With the FTP client software, open a new connection. The FTP client will ask for the user name, location and password of an FTP account. New web hosting accounts often provide an FTP account, but if not you will need to create one with your own user name and password. Each FTP account points to a specific directory on your web hosting account. It usually works best to have the FTP account point to your public web directory like 'public_html' so that any file you upload to that directory will be available on the Internet.

Creating Simple Web Pages

Web pages are files containing plain text and special HTML tags. Following is an example of a simple web page:

```
<html>
    <head>
        <title>My first web page</title>
    </head>
    <body>
        Hello there!
    </body>
</html>
```

HTML tags usually come in pairs. For example, the text between <title> and </title> is the page title. The <html> and </html> pair defines the beginning and end of the document. Information about the web page is located between the <head> tags, and the content of the web page is found between the <body> tags. In a web browser, this web page will display the message 'Hello there!', and the title 'My first web page' will appear in the tab above the page.

There are nearly a hundred different HTML tags. Some of the more common tags include the tags <h1> for major headings and <p> for paragraphs of text:

```
<h1>Introduction</h1>
<p>This is a paragraph of text.</p>
```

A link to another web page uses the <a> tag:

```
<a href="http://jpedia.org">Visit
the home page of JP Allen.</a>
```

The text 'Visit the home page of JP Allen.' will display as underlined text on a web page. If that text is clicked on, the visitor will be taken to jpedia.org. The 'href' inside of the tag is an *attribute*, or a piece of additional information for the HTML tag. In this case, the HTML tag needs to know where a visitor should go if the text is clicked on.

An image can be added to a web page using the <img> tag:

```
<img alt="JP with Chicken" width="480"
height="640" src="http://jpedia.org/
jpchicken.jpeg" >
```

For this HTML tag to work, the image must be available on the Internet at the URL specified in the 'src' attribute, or http://jpedia.org/jpchicken.jpeg. If the image is not available online at that URL, the web page will display a broken image. The 'width' and 'height' attributes are expressed as numbers of pixels on a screen, and the 'alt' attribute is the alternative text displayed if images cannot be shown. The 'alt', 'width', and 'height' attributes in this example are all optional; without them, the web browser will show the picture in its original size and with no alternative text.

A web page can be created in any text editor by writing, copying, and pasting text and HTML tags. If the HTML document is saved as a plain text file with a file name ending in. htm or. html, then the web page can be uploaded to a web host in the same way as the image example earlier. Web page editor programs such as Adobe Creative Suite or the free BlueGriffon make it easier to create web pages without memorizing HTML tags.

Adding Style Sheet Rules to a Web Page

Web pages written only in HTML are pretty boring to look at. To add colors, new fonts, and to control where things appear on a screen designers use style sheet rules written in a language called CSS (Cascading Style Sheets). CSS rules can change the way content contained in an HTML tag will appear. For example, the CSS rules below would change the text between <h1> tags to display at 22-point font size and centered and change the text between <p> tags to display as 14-point font size and blue:

```
h1 {font-size:22pt; text-align:center;}
p {font-size:14pt; color:blue;}
```

There are dozens of different CSS properties, such as 'font-size' and 'color' that can be used to change the look and feel of a web page without changing the content.

The <div> tag in HTML and a CSS id can be used to change the appearance of any part of a web page. For example, the CSS rule

```
#bluebox {border:2px blue solid;}
```

will change the appearance of any content between the <div> tags using a matching 'id' attribute, as shown below:

```
<div id="bluebox">
    Content here is surrounded by a
    blue border.
</div>
```

CSS style sheet rules can be added to a web page by placing them between a <style> and a </style> tag, which in turn should be placed between the <head> and </head> tag of an HTML document. The CSS rules can also be written in a separate file with a filename ending in. css. If a CSS file is available on the Internet at http://jpedia.org/style.css then the following <link> tag can be placed within the <head> of an HTML document:

```
<link href="http://jpedia.org/style.css"
rel="stylesheet" type="text/css">
```

Using Content Management Software for Prototypes

More than half of all web sites today use content management system (CMS) software to create and manage their sites. Instead of custom coding web pages, content management software automatically handles the details of generating web pages. Content management software will install a web site at a specific web address (URL), and allow the owner to log in, add content, change the look and feel, and add new features without having to change the underlying HTML or CSS code. Content management software is a powerful tool for creating digital prototypes that can serve real customers.

The most popular CMS by far, WordPress, is used by 31% of all web sites at the time of writing. Joomla (3%) and Drupal (2%) are two other popular free software choices for managing web sites, followed by the paid services Squarespace (1%) and Shopify (1%). Incredibly, even though WordPress is the market leader and used by many of the largest corporations, the software is completely free to use and modify. As the market leader, WordPress has the largest ecosystem, which means having the most freely available add-ons and the most active developer and user communities. For these reasons, WordPress is the CMS used for prototyping in this book, but many of the same principles apply to other CMSs.

Free WordPress sites are available by setting up an account at wordpress.com, but these sites are owned by wordpress.com and are limited in the number of new features than can be added. Because the software itself is free, we will instead install a WordPress site on our own server using a web hosting account, and maintain full control and ownership of our business prototypes without much additional work.

Installing a New (Empty) Prototype Site on a Web Host Using WordPress

Most web hosting services make it easy to create a new WordPress site. After logging in to a web hosting account, there is usually an option to 'install WordPress', or perhaps an option to do 'one-click installs' or 'install software', after which WordPress can be chosen.

The most important decision for a new WordPress installation is where it should be located. A WordPress site can be installed at a domain, such as jpedia.org, or within a subdirectory, such as jpedia.org/blog. An installation at jpedia.org will copy the hundreds of files that make up a new WordPress site into the public web directory for that domain, such as 'public_html'. An installation at jpedia.org/blog will create a new directory called 'blog' within the public web directory for jpedia.org and copy all the WordPress files into the 'blog' directory. Only one WordPress installation can be in one folder—don't install more than one WordPress site in the same location!—but WordPress installations in different folders can be completely different web sites, with different content and different looks.

Once a new WordPress site is installed, you will be given two URLs, or web addresses. One URL is the address of the WordPress site itself as it appears to the outside world. Visit this URL in a web browser and make sure the site is working. It will be empty at first, with a simple 'Hello World' message and generic image. The other

URL will be the administrator log in page. By browsing to this location and entering the administrator user name and password, you will be able to change the web site's content and settings. Make sure you are able to log in to your new WordPress site as an administrator and see the 'Dashboard' for your site. From the 'Settings' menu, under 'General' you will find some of the generic settings for your site such as the site title and tag line.

WordPress in general is fairly tolerant of beginners jumping in and playing around with settings and commands. One important exception is the URL or address of the site, found under 'Settings' → 'General'. Do not change this URL; otherwise the software will look for your site in the wrong place and you will likely be locked out of your own site. Under the 'Tools' menu is an export setting to save your site content in case something goes horribly wrong. Web hosting accounts often include site backup tools, or there are backup plugins that can be added to WordPress sites to give you peace of mind as you play around with the technology (adding plugins will be discussed in Chapter 7).

Congratulations! If you made it this far, you have traveled from the details of IP addresses and web pages to the creation of a starter web site prototype with incredible untapped power. Try the exercises before you proceed, and use the step-by-step guide in the appendix to measure your progress on the journey to a full digital business prototype.

Additional Resources

www.w3schools.com/—resource for HTML and CSS
    languages.
www.bluegriffon.org/—free software for editing web pages.

https://my.bluehost.com/hosting/help/432—example of how to modify nameservers for a domain name.

https://my.bluehost.com/hosting/help/cyberduck—example of how to set up FTP.

https://my.bluehost.com/hosting/help/wordpress—example of how to install a new web site using WordPress software.

https://cyberduck.io/—free FTP client software.

https://filezilla-project.org/—free FTP client software.

www.siteground.com/studentsprogram—web hosting service with student discounts.

www.bluehost.com/hosting/education—web hosting service with student discounts.

https://wordpress.org/showcase/—example WordPress web sites.

https://codex.wordpress.org/Getting_Started_with_WordPress—official WordPress documentation and help pages.

https://wordpress.org/themes/—official directory of free WordPress themes.

https://wordpress.org/plugins/—official directory of free WordPress plugins.

https://w3techs.com/technologies/history_overview/content_management/all—data on content management systems market share.

Exercises

4.1. Find two available domain names for a digital business idea. Ask three other people for their feedback on which domain name would be best for your idea.

4.2. Sign up for a web hosting service and successfully log on to the web hosting account.

4.3. Create a simple web page, available at your own domain name, that can be viewed through another person's web browser. The web page should include an image, a link to another web page, and two style sheet rules.

4.4. Install a new WordPress website on your domain. Log in to the administrator 'dashboard' and view the new site in a web browser.

4.5. Change the settings of a WordPress site, such as site title, to reflect your digital business idea.

References

[1] B. Schwerdt, *How to Build an Online Business*. Milton, Queensland: John Wiley & Sons, 2018.

[2] D. Ryan, *Understanding Digital Marketing: Marketing Strategies for Engaging the Digital Generation*. London: Kogan Page Publishers, 2016.

[3] A. W. West, *Practical Web Design for Absolute Beginners*. Colyton: Apress, 2016.

Digital Content for Business

Highlights

Chapter 5 introduces digital content as a powerful tool that digital entrepreneurs can use to attract and satisfy customers.

- A content strategy for a digital business includes decisions about content creation, delivery, and ongoing maintenance.

- Content management software makes it easy to add and update content on digital prototypes. This chapter shows how to add and organize content using the most popular content management software, WordPress, but the same principles apply to other software as well.

- Digital content can be categorized to make it more useful for potential customers, and easier to find.

- Content is made accessible on digital prototypes through navigation structures such as menus and links between pages.

Content Strategy

Digital entrepreneurs have an advantage over their non-digital counterparts in one respect—they can use digital content to attract and satisfy customers. There are many different types of digital content:

- Different *topics*: limited only by the imagination.

- Different technical *formats*: text, images, videos, or audio.

- Different *genres*: stories, updates, brochures, newsletters, technical information, white papers, interviews, success stories, instructional videos, ultrashort videos, interactive quizzes, infographics, or memes.

- Different *frequencies*: multiple updates per day, daily, weekly, or as needed.

Any content that is useful or entertaining, or both can become a business tool. Even the most obscure topic can find a following online. Content is critical for search placement and for social media engagement. Because of the importance of digital content, having a deliberate content strategy can be helpful in the initial prototype building and for maintaining a steady stream of content production over the longer term. A content strategy helps ensure that content is deliberately targeted for business needs.

Content strategy is 'planning for the creation, delivery, and governance of useful, usable content' [1]. Content creation includes decisions about what content will be created, where it will come from, and how it will be organized. Content delivery is about who will approve of new content, and where and how it will be uploaded. Content governance includes the policies and standards for evaluating content and for deciding which content needs to be updated or removed.

When starting a new digital business prototype, beginners often get sidetracked by how a site looks.

While it's understandable that a budding entrepreneur would want their site to look great, the right content is usually a better source of conversions than good looks. The more quickly a reasonable amount and variety of content is made available on a prototype, the faster that experimentation can begin. Providing high quality content in a sustainable manner is one of the best ways to help a new digital business idea succeed. For some digital business ideas, unique content essentially is the business.

Content Creation

The first part of a content strategy answers the key content creation questions: What content will be created and why? Where will it come from? And how will it be organized?

What content will be created is a question of defining the topic. The main topic of the content should come naturally from the digital business idea. For a specific topic, there are usually multiple ways to specialize within it, with some phrasings or angles that are more popular than others. A quick search on a tool such as Google Trends can reveal if any phrases related to your topic are rising in popularity [2].

The answer to the why question for content is some combination of the PIE elements: *Persuasive* content that makes a direct argument for your product or service; *Informative* content that educates customers and provides useful information; and *Entertaining* content that, well, entertains. Finding the right combination is a relatively new business problem for which there is not yet a lot of guidance and hard data.

The most research has been done on persuasive content, where standard marketing advice applies. Sell a benefit or a dream, not a product. Any page a visitor can arrive at should make a clear and obvious offer to a potential customer and have an obvious way to convert.

Even the words used can make a difference. One expert advises using short, active words and sentences and using the present tense rather than future so that customers can visualize that a sale or transaction has already happened [3]. A simpler offer might use minimal text, while a more complex product or service might benefit from longer text forms or longer videos [4]. Where the persuasive content is shared can also affect content size. One study found that 890 seconds was the highest performing video length on YouTube, while 81 seconds was the best amount of time on Facebook [5].

Finding the most effective informative and entertaining content will likely require experimenting. For informative and educational content, the digital world rewards content with a clear hook that grabs attention away from other competing sources and is structured so that it can easily be scanned—as seen in the popular list format of Internet articles and step-by-step how-to articles.

Just like news articles, online content can be written in an inverted pyramid format, where the main takeaway and argument comes first and the details are revealed later. A more informal, conversational style might be more effective online, even for serious content [5]. For business-to-business (B2B) selling, content marketing is moving away from a pure sales or persuasion approach to more of a 'helping' approach that shows customers how they can have successful results using your product or service [6].

The second question to answer in content creation strategy is where content will come from. Content can be original, it can be made under contract or license, or it can be collected and aggregated from elsewhere. For a community-based digital business, content can be generated by users. Depending on the size and complexity of the content, content creation might require a defined process or workflow. Quick status updates or blog posts might have a simple process, such as writing and then a quick edit. More complex writing, such as white papers and customer success stories, will need to include research and fact-checking steps.

More demanding formats such as video might require pre-production and post-production activities such as location and talent scouting, editing, graphics design, and finding equipment and production crews. Don't assume that quality content magically appears. The biggest benefits from good content come when content is regularly updated. Customers are less likely to trust stale, inactive businesses, and search engines are less likely to highlight businesses that don't regularly update their content.

The third content creation question is how content will be organized. For a prototype web site, a good starting point is to draw up a basic information architecture that shows how the first five to ten pages are connected. The initial pages might all be at the same level, or some could be grouped together underneath the top-level pages to form the beginning of a site hierarchy. Proper organization also includes the correct metadata, or data about the content. At a minimum, metadata includes a title and description that will help the content be found in a search, but can also include category labels for related content that might keep visitors on site and engaged for a longer period of time.

Content Delivery

The delivery aspect of content strategy answers questions about who will approve new content, and where and how it will be uploaded. For digital businesses that create or license original content, delivery starts with the entrepreneur deciding which content to try and uploading it to a prototype site themselves.

For businesses that depend on communities to create content, decisions need to be made about moderation. Will community members be allowed to post content and have it appear on a site immediately, removing it afterwards only if there is a problem? Or will all comments and uploads require pre-approval from a moderator? Fortunately, content management software makes it easy to set policies for moderation and quickly review and approve content for site posting. As a digital business grows, however, moderation will become increasingly time consuming.

Where and how content will be uploaded is a fairly easy question to answer in the early stages of business prototyping. The details of how to add and organize content on a WordPress prototype will be covered next. If content will be updated regularly at additional online locations, such as social media profiles, then the content may need to be summarized or shortened for other uses. As a digital business grows, content can be uploaded to a specialized Content Delivery Network (or CDN) that speeds up the delivery of content by keeping multiple copies in different parts of the world.

Content Governance

Content governance includes any policies or standards for evaluating how effective content is, and for deciding which content needs to be updated or removed. Digital content requires constant maintenance, particularly as it grows, or else ineffective and outdated content will gradually take over a digital business and distract visitors away from the high quality content that leads to conversions.

Governance for a new digital business prototype starts with a commitment to regularly evaluate each piece of content uploaded. Content performance is normally evaluated in terms of the conversion rate it produces, but might also be evaluated by engagement measures such the number of views or shares. Basic information that does not change much, such as contact information for a promotion business, may not need to be evaluated often. But even content that might be considered stable, such as the 'About Us' story of a business, would benefit from regular performance review. If a business already has a substantial amount of content, then an audit that catalogs all available content is a useful first step.

Adding Content to Prototypes

Content management software such as WordPress makes it easy to add content to a prototype site. The software even keeps tracks of different versions, so that unwanted changes can be undone later. The first step for adding content is to choose a content type. WordPress has two default content types: *pages* and *posts*. A page is a standard web page, displayed one at a time at its own URL. A post is a blog article with a specific publication time and date. All posts are displayed on a single page, with the newest post at the top. A typical prototype site uses both pages and posts: pages for the information that isn't time sensitive, such as an 'about us' page or a 'contact us' page, and posts for news items or blog articles.

To create a new page, go to the 'Pages' menu from the administrator area of your WordPress site and select 'Add New'. Fill in the title of the page, which will be used as part of the URL for the page. WordPress provides a nice editor for creating the page without having to know HTML tags. Pages are made by creating a series of 'Blocks', each of which can contain text, an image, or other kinds of standard content such as image galleries, files, YouTube videos, or Twitter tweets. Blocks can be added by clicking on a '+' sign with a circle around it either on the page or in the upper left corner of the screen. Blocks can be rearranged by dragging and dropping.

If HTML code needs to be edited on a page, select a block and choose from the options menu above it 'Edit as HMTL'. Or choose 'Code Editor' from the options menu on the upper right of the screen. Once editing is complete, the page is saved as a draft. The page is only made available to the public when the blue 'Publish' button is clicked.

Create a page for the digital business prototype and visit its URL (shown above the title, when the title is selected) to make sure you understand where to find it. Notice that when a visitor sees a page, they see not only the title and content you have created, but also headers, footers, menus, and perhaps sidebars around your page content. The content management software automatically fills in those other areas of the screen. The next chapter discusses how to manage these parts of the screen by customizing the layout, or theme, of a WordPress site.

Back at the page editing screen, available through the WordPress administrator area by selecting the 'Posts' menu, then 'All Posts', then clicking on a post to edit, additional information about the page can be seen in the 'Settings' column on the right side of the screen (if empty, click on the gear icon at the upper right of the screen). For example, the option for whether comments are allowed on a page is set under the 'Document' tab at 'Discussion'.

To create a new post, the process is similar. Go to the 'Posts' menu from the WordPress administrator area and select 'Add New'. A similar editing page will appear, but with slightly different options in the 'Settings' column on the right. For example, an 'Excerpt' option can be used to create a short description of a post, which will hopefully convince a reader to click through and read an entire article. Click on the blue 'Publish' button to make the post available to readers.

The 'Front' page, or 'Home' page, is the page that visitors are taken to if they ask for a domain name rather than a specific page (for example, if they ask for jpedia.org, rather than the more specific jpedia.org/about_us.html). By default, WordPress will show posts on the front page with the most recent posts on top. For many businesses, it makes more sense to have a home page that doesn't change every time a new post is created. WordPress calls this a 'static' front page.

To change the front page, from the WordPress administrator area go to 'Settings', then 'Reading'. Under 'Front Page Displays', choose a 'Static page', then select one of the pages already created to be the front page.

Once the posts are no longer displayed on the front page, they will need to appear on some other page. Create a new blank page, called 'News', 'Blog', or some other name appropriate for your business and set that blank page as the 'Posts page'.

Organizing Content

After creating an initial set of pages and posts, the next step is to arrange that content in useful ways. Posts in WordPress are assigned to one or more categories or to a special category called 'uncategorized' if no assignment is made. A good set of categories will organize posts in ways that potential customers are likely to look for information. Categories are especially useful as the amount of content grows. When a visitor finds one post they like, categories will let them find similar items that will encourage them to read more, deepening their engagement with the business. Well thought out categories also give visitors important clues about the purpose and benefits of a business. If more than five to ten categories are needed, consider creating subcategories. Posts can also be labeled with tags, which are typically used more like the specific terms in an index rather than broad categories.

Pages are organized through their navigation structure, which includes the links between pages and the site menus. The WordPress page editor makes it easy to create a link from one page to any other. On the page editor screen, click the 'insert link' button when a block of text is selected—it looks like a paper clip. The insert link button can add a link to any URL on the Internet, or it can automatically create a link to any other page already published on the site.

Menus are a consistently formatted set of links that visitors expect to find at the top of every page, and perhaps at the sides and bottom also depending on the layout. Many WordPress themes automatically create a main menu by including links to every page in alphabetical order, but business prototypes should replace this default menu with their own.

The process for creating a menu in WordPress is to first create a new menu, then add 'Items' or individual links to a menu, and finally assign the menu to a location on the screen. From the WordPress administrator area, go to the 'Appearance' menu, then 'Menus', then 'Create a new menu'.

Once a new menu is named and saved, items can be added. Most items will be pages, but WordPress also allows the adding of posts, categories of posts, or any Internet URL as a menu item. The menu items can be dragged and dropped to rearrange their order and to create submenus. The final step is to assign a menu to a 'Theme location'. Each theme, or layout, will have its own set of locations on the screen where a menu can be placed. For the main menu, there is usually an option called the 'Primary' or 'Main' menu, and that is where the first menu should be placed. Save the changes and check the prototype site to see if the new menu appears.

By now, your business prototype may not look too exciting, but it should have five to ten pages of content, a few posts, and a main menu. Together with a content strategy for regular evaluation and updating, your business prototype is already better than many existing small business sites that suffer from outdated content and poor organization. The next step is what you're dying to do anyway, and that is make your business prototype look and feel great.

Additional Resources

www.usability.gov/what-and-why/content-strategy.html—
overview of content strategy.

https://codex.wordpress.org/Pages—how to add pages in
WordPress.

https://codex.wordpress.org/Writing_Posts—how to add
posts in WordPress.

https://codex.wordpress.org/Creating_a_Static_Front_Page—
how to set the front page in WordPress.

www.wpbeginner.com/beginners-guide/categories-vs-tags-
seo-best-practices-which-one-is-better/—categorization
tips for WordPress posts.

www.wpbeginner.com/beginners-guide/beginners-guide-
on-how-to-add-a-link-in-wordpress/#linkvisualeditor—
adding links to pages and posts.

https://codex.wordpress.org/WordPress_Menu_User_Guide—
creating and activating a new menu in WordPress.

www.toprankblog.com/2018/05/b2b-content-marketing-case-
studies-2018/—collection of short content marketing
case studies.

Exercises

5.1. Find three different examples of effective content
online related to your digital business idea. Describe
their topic, technical format, genre, and if possible,
the frequency of updating. Discuss what makes this
content effective.

5.2. Define the content creation strategy for your digital
business idea. Include a description of what content
will be created, with what purpose or purposes, and
where it will come from.

5.3. Define the content delivery and governance strategy
for your digital business. Include the decisions about

moderation, updating frequency, and frequency of performance review.

5.4. Add the first five pages to your digital business prototype. Check all content for errors.

5.5. Create a set of five to ten categories for your digital business prototype.

5.6. Design the main navigational menu for your digital business prototype. Create the menu and assign it to a screen location.

5.7. Add at least two posts to your digital business prototype with news, offers, or commentaries relevant to your digital business idea. Categorize the posts.

References

[1] K. Halvorson and M. Rach, *Content Strategy for the Web*. Berkeley, CA: New Riders, 2012.

[2] F. Alhlou, S. Asif, and E. Fettman, *Google Analytics Breakthrough: From Zero to Business Impact*. Hoboken, NJ: John Wiley & Sons, 2016.

[3] D. Croxen-John and J. van Tonder, *E-Commerce Website Optimization: Why 95 Per Cent of Your Webiste Visitors Don't Buy and What You Can Do About It*. London: Kogan Page, 2017.

[4] P. Marshall, K. Krance, and T. Meloche, *Ultimate Guide to Facebook Advertising: How to Access 1 Billion Potential Customers in 10 Minutes*, 2nd ed. Irvine, CA: Entrepreneur Press, 2015.

[5] D. Ryan, *Understanding* Digital *Marketing: Marketing Strategies for Engaging the Digital Generation*. London: Kogan Page Publishers, 2016.

[6] G. Holliman and J. Rowley, "Business to Business Digital Content Marketing: Marketers' Perceptions of Best Practice," *Journal of Research in Interactive Marketing*, vol. 8, no. 4, pp. 269–293, 2014.

Business Prototype Look and Feel

Highlights

Chapter 6 introduces the basics of user interface design for business prototyping.

- Providing a great user experience is critical for digital business. The user interface of a site defines how it looks and feels to a potential customer.

- Content management software uses themes (also known as templates) to define the look and feel of a site.

- Using themes allows a digital entrepreneur to create a professional looking site quickly and makes it easier to change the appearance of a site without modifying existing content.

- Themes define screen layouts, or a common structure for web pages on a site. Some areas of a screen layout are filled automatically with content, while other areas can usually be configured or edited.

- By the end of this chapter, the reader should be able to select a theme for a digital prototype, install a theme on a prototype site, and customize the theme for a digital business idea.

User Experience and User Interface Design

The digital world creates opportunities for entrepreneurs to build a better product or service through new kinds of user experience. User experience (or UX) is how a customer experiences a product or service in real world use, including a customer's feelings or emotional reactions [1].

UX goes beyond the features and appearance of a product to include how it is used in real world situations. For example, there are many different ways to design an alarm clock or a coffee maker that do the same basic job. But how many buttons should there be? How well will a shape fit on a typical bedside table or kitchen counter? Simple products don't have as many design choices, but the more complex a product or service, the more user experience choices need to be made. (Simplicity of user experience is another reason for keeping business prototypes as minimal as possible.)

User experience is challenging in the digital world because of the number of different design and action possibilities on even the simplest web pages. Most customers will interact with a digital business as a self-service product, without a lot of obvious help available. UX also includes any interactions with a business outside of a web page, including requests for help or support.

The UX challenge is also an opportunity for digital entrepreneurs to create a better product or service than what exists today. *Ease of use* is the ability of customers to achieve their goals without unnecessary effort or frustration. Even small design changes can make a difference. Something as simple as a different color, size, or location for a 'buy now' button can lead to a more satisfying experience and a higher conversion rate.

One important aspect of user experience is user interface (UI) design. The user interface of a web site is how a person interacts with a site. As discussed in earlier chapters, web pages separate the content of pages, coded in HTML, from how that content is presented on a screen, with rules coded in CSS. The look and feel of a business prototype will be determined mostly by the CSS rules, whether we write them ourselves or use themes or templates designed by others.

User Interface Design: Guidelines

Finding the right user interface design for a digital business will likely take time and experimenting, but there are good guidelines to start with [2]. Four basic principles for user interface design are minimalism, consistency, real world language, and focused help.

Minimalism—in user interface design, less is often more. A visitor comes to a site with a goal in mind, and a clean, minimalist design is more likely to make it clear what can be accomplished and how. A minimalist look does not distract or confuse a customer. A clean look makes it more obvious what the main purpose of each page is and where to find things. Excessive text, too many images, weird or hard to read color schemes, and unclear navigation are common problems that minimalism helps fight against.

Consistency—customers tend to leave a digital business when they are confused about how and where to find things. Consistency means that menus and options are named consistently and are always found in the same place throughout a site, reducing confusion and frustration.

Real world language—using language that makes sense to customers, rather than technical terms, helps reduce confusion and frustration. Don't use terms like 'posts', 'pages', or 'uploads' unless they are commonly understood by your audience. The labels for menu options are a great opportunity to explain to customers in their own language what can be done on a site and what the benefits might be for them.

Focused help—customers visiting a web page are mostly on their own when it comes to assistance. If a digital business is asking a customer to go through a multi-step process such as filling in a profile to sign up for a service, then the user interface should offer help that is focused on the task they are trying to achieve and provide step-by-step guidance. Additional 'how it works' information can be placed on a popular front page, included on a separate 'help' page, or both.

Changing Prototype Look and Feel

Content management software such as WordPress uses themes to define how a site looks and feels. Themes contain the CSS rules that define colors, fonts, screen layout, and other aspects of how a business prototype will appear. As the most popular open content management software, WordPress has thousands of freely available pre-defined themes to choose from. The official collection of free WordPress themes can be found at wordpress.org/themes. Using themes allows a prototype builder to create a professional looking site quickly. The appearance of a site can be changed without fear of messing up the content and can be easily undone.

To change the theme of a WordPress site, log on to the administrator area and choose the 'Appearance' menu on the left, then 'Themes'. A new WordPress site will have two or three standard themes to choose from. A theme can be previewed to see what it will look like, or it can be activated to become the live theme for the site. Additional themes can be added from the official WordPress theme collection by clicking on the 'Add new theme' box. Themes can also be downloaded from other sources, then added to a site manually by uploading the theme to a special directory called 'wp-content/themes' within the WordPress installation on your web hosting service.

With so many themes to choose from, choosing the right theme can be a guessing game at first. Themes with more downloads and that are updated regularly are likely to be higher quality. Some themes are quite basic with few options, while others have many customization possibilities. Many themes use responsive CSS technology, meaning that they automatically adjust their screen layout depending on the width of the screen, adjusting the user interface to be more effective for phones, tablets, and other smaller touch screen devices.

Because it is easy to switch between themes, install three or four popular ones on a prototype site and try them out. Most themes are image heavy, so unless you already have a set of high-quality images ready to go your prototype may not look as beautiful as the example sites in their documentation. Getting the most out of themes, particularly complex themes, will require some customization.

Theme Customization

The currently active theme for a site can be customized by selecting 'Appearance' from the left side menu in the administration area, then 'Customize', or by clicking the 'Customize' button on the theme listing screen. The left side menu contains the customization options for the active theme. Each theme has its own customization choices, some more than others. If the theme is not allowing you to customize something that is important to your design it might be time to try a different theme.

One of the standard WordPress themes, called 'Twenty Seventeen', has a typical set of customization settings. 'Site Identity' allows the site title and tagline to be changed and a site logo to be uploaded.

The 'Twenty Seventeen' theme offers a few different color options under 'Colors', but not many customization options compared with other themes. Under 'Header Media', the header image can be easily customized by uploading an image to replace the default picture of a potted cactus. In this theme, the header image covers most of what a visitor will see on the front page, so the selection of a high-quality picture that will convey the purpose and benefit of the site to potential customers is vital—visitors will have few other visual aids to help them figure out what the site is about.

Featuring a large image on a site's front page is known as a *hero image*. Hero images have become popular in site design because visitors often relate more strongly to, or are more intrigued by, beautiful images rather than text, but this is one of many look and feel assumptions that can be tested in the course of building a business prototype. A large image on the front page may look great, for example, but it might make it harder for a visitor to find a call to action.

Once customization choices are made, click on the blue 'Publish' button to save the changes and make them active. Customization changes only apply to a specific theme. If a new theme is activated, the customization settings of the old theme will not apply, but they will be restored if the old theme is activated again.

Screen Layout

Themes define a consistent screen layout that is used on most pages of a site. Often there is a header area at the top of the screen. Then there is a main content area, with perhaps a sidebar area to the left or right of it and a footer area at the bottom. The screen layout will also define where menus can be placed. For example, the 'Twenty Seventeen' theme has two screen areas where menus can be located, one at the top of the screen below the header image and one at the bottom of the footer for 'social' links. Displaying a menu in different locations will reveal where menus can be placed in a theme.

Themes also use 'Widgets' in WordPress to display standard pieces of content on every page, typically in a sidebar or in a footer. Widgets are useful for consistently displaying a call to action on every page, an advertisement, or any piece of information that is important enough to appear across multiple pages. Widgets can also be used for navigation, such as adding another menu in a sidebar or displaying categories of posts. Standard WordPress widgets include an audio player, a calendar, an image gallery, recent posts or comments, and a video player. The 'Custom HTML' widget is useful for cutting and pasting any HTML web code and having it appear across all pages of a site.

The important thing digital entrepreneurs need to understand about screen layout is knowing which parts of the screen are content that can be edited as a web page, which parts of the screen can be changed through theme customization, and which parts are fixed by a theme and cannot be changed without modifying theme code. Once it is clear what goes where on a screen and how to customize themes, the entrepreneur has control over their prototype's look and feel.

Advanced Theme Customization: Changing the Code

If a theme isn't looking and feeling the way it should even after customization, then the standard advice is to look for a different theme. (Or, even better, stop obsessing about site appearance and get an MVP out quickly for customer feedback.) But sometimes everything is right about a theme except for one little thing—a font size here, or a color there—and there's no customization option to change it. In these situations, it might be useful to change or add CSS rules to a site's theme.

In principle, because WordPress is entirely open source software and it is installed on your own hosting server, you can change the actual code of your prototype site at any time. Exploratory edits of raw code are likely to lead to disaster for the uninitiated, however, so a better option is to use the 'Additional CSS' option in theme customizing.

Recall from Chapter 4 that CSS code starts with a selector, such as 'p' for all content contained between

HTML paragraph or <p> tags, followed by the style rules that apply to all the content defined by the selector. For example, the following rule changes all paragraph text to 14-point font, and blue:

```
p {font-size:14pt; color:blue;}
```

In addition to rules for HTML tags, CSS code can also define its own selectors, so that different CSS rules can apply to different pieces of content. We learned before about defining a CSS id, and then using the <div> tag to apply the CSS rules to specific content. For example:

```
<div id="bluebox">
     Content here is surrounded by a blue
     border.
</div>
#bluebox {border:2px blue solid;}
```

WordPress themes normally use a class rather than an id for the same thing. To set rules using classes, the HTML and CSS code will look something like this if we wanted to make a particular paragraph white color:

```
<p class="site-description">
     Your site tagline here.
</p>
.site-description {color:white;}
```

The main difficulty in adding CSS code is finding the right selector for a particular screen element that needs to be changed. CSS can define general rules such as the background image for the header part of the screen and at the same time more specific rules that override some of the rules in certain circumstances, such as a different font color for only the tagline text within the header. This is very useful (the 'Cascading' part of CSS) for not constantly repeating CSS rules and keeping them consistent, but it can be confusing to find the right selector when the content to be changed is nested within three or four sets of rules.

For example, to change the font color of the site title to purple and capitalization to mixed case in the 'Twenty Seventeen' theme when using an image header, we would add the following to 'Additional CSS':

```
body.has-header-image. site-title
a{color:purple; text-transform:
capitalize;}
```

The complicated selector includes a class '.site-title' within a larger class '.has-header-image', and only applies to links using the HTML <a> tag. Web browsers such as Firefox and Chrome have developer tools that allow designers to click on parts of a web page and find the exact CSS rules that apply, including the selectors. An easier method is to use a WordPress plugin such as 'SiteOrigin CSS', which allows designers to point and click at parts of the screen and add CSS rules without knowing the exact selectors. Installing most plugins is easy and will be covered in the next chapter.

CSS can feel a bit crazy at the beginning but does offer a lot of power. As another example, sometimes it would be more professional to remove certain parts of a theme for business use. CSS can be used to make an element visible or not without changing any of the underlying code. For example, to remove the standard 'Powered by WordPress' message in the footer of the 'Twenty Seventeen' theme this rule can be added to 'Additional CSS', hiding all content within the class 'site-info':

```
.site-info{visibility:hidden;}
```

No matter how much customization is done, the main message for digital entrepreneurs is that content management software like WordPress makes it easy to create prototype digital business sites that look and feel great. The next step will be to not just change the looks of a prototype, but to add new features and functions.

Additional Resources

www.nngroup.com/articles/definition-user-experience/ — good definition of user experience.

https://wordpress.org/themes/ — official source for free WordPress themes.

https://codex.wordpress.org/Using_Themes — help for how to use WordPress themes, and how they work.

www.codeinwp.com/blog/free-wordpress-business-themes/ — an example of one of many articles reviewing free WordPress themes for business sites.

https://codex.wordpress.org/Appearance_Customize_Screen — help for using theme customization in WordPress.

https://envato.com/blog/exploring-hero-image-trend-web-design/ — discussion of the power of large 'hero images' on web site front pages.

https://wordpress.org/plugins/so-css/ — home page for the SiteOrigin CSS plugin which makes it easier to add CSS rules to a site.

Exercises

6.1. Find two promising free themes for your business prototype in the official WordPress themes directory. Try both themes on a prototype site and show them to at one other person. Which theme do you prefer, and why?

6.2. List the top three ways in which you would like to change the look and feel of a prototype site.

Discuss whether theme customization will be good enough or if a new theme will need to be found.

6.3. On a piece of paper, draw the names and locations of the screen areas as defined by the active theme on your prototype site.

6.4. Add at least two widgets to your business prototype that are appropriate for your digital business idea.

6.5. Review the entire look and feel of a business prototype. Check that all areas of your screen serve a business purpose and that nothing will cause potential customers to be confused or lose trust in your business.

References

[1]   J. J. Garrett, *The Elements of User Experience: User-Centered Design for the Web and Beyond, Second Edition*. Berkeley, California: New Riders, 2010.

[2]   J. Nielsen. *10 Usability Heuristics for User Interface Design*. (1995), available: www.nngroup.com/articles/ten-usability-heuristics/. [Accessed: July 14, 2018].

Business Prototype Features

Highlights

Chapter 7 shows how to choose, install, and configure a wide range of additional features on WordPress prototypes through the use of plugins.

- An important benefit of using content management software for prototypes is the ability to add new features without having to code. The leading software platforms have many freely available add-ons.

- New add-ons include *front-end features* that customers interact with, such as a contact form; *back-end features* that work behind the scenes, such as providing additional security protection; and *integration features* that connect to other Internet services, such as a Twitter feed or a map.

- By adding features, general purpose content management software can be used to create specialized prototypes for different types of digital business including content and community businesses, online stores, matchmaking businesses, and promotion businesses.

- By the end of the chapter, the reader should be able to add new features on to their prototypes, including installation and configuration.

Adding New Features to a Prototype

Web pages are wonderful for displaying content, but HTML tags and CSS rules only provide limited types of interactions with customers. Confirming that a visitor has the correct password, displaying a changing Instagram feed, or completing a credit card purchase are all examples of interactions that require additional software code to make decisions and adapt to changing situations. Web pages with only HTML content and CSS rules that display the same information every time they are requested are called *static* pages. Web pages generated with the help of additional code are *dynamic* in the sense that the content of a page can change depending on circumstances and previously stored information [1].

Content management software such as WordPress creates dynamic pages using a coding language called PHP [2]. When a web page is requested, the PHP code will run on a server, which will perform its calculations and output the requested page. A person requesting the web page will only see the resulting HTML and CSS, not the PHP code that generated it.

Additional code that runs within a user's web browser, written in a programming language called Javascript, is also used by WordPress to add more interactivity to web pages [3]. Javascript can change the appearance of a web page based on user inputs and information available through a user's web browser. PHP is an example of *server-side* code, while Javascript is an example of *client-side* code.

WordPress provides a basic set of features for content management: users signing in and out, adding pages and posts, creating menus, and customizing themes. New pieces of code that add additional features are called *plugins*. As the most popular open content management software, WordPress has an incredible universe of tens of thousands of available plugins that are partially or entirely free to use. For the digital entrepreneur, plugins are a way to add new code and new features to a prototype site without being a programmer. Entrepreneurs can experiment by trying new features themselves as they learn more about customer needs.

Installing plugins can be a little more complex than changing themes, especially if a plugin connects to outside services such as a Google map or a Facebook login. The objective of this chapter is to show how to select, install, and configure a range of typical plugins for WordPress business prototype sites.

How to Install WordPress Plugins

As a first example, let's install a plugin called 'GTranslate' that will use Google Translate to automatically provide language translation for our prototype site. From the WordPress administrative area, select 'Plugins' on the left, then 'Add New'. Type 'gtranslate' into the search box on the upper right. One of the first results should be the 'Translate WordPress with GTranslate' plugin. Click on 'Install Now', then 'Activate'.

Activating the 'GTranslate' plugin hasn't changed anything on the prototype site yet, from the customer point of view. The plugin has done two things on the administrator side, however. First, it has added a new option to the 'Settings' menu called 'GTranslate'. Selecting this option will show the configuration choices available for a new translation widget that can be added to the prototype. Choose how the widget will look at the top, the languages you wish to include, and click 'Save Changes' at the bottom.

The second thing added by the plugin is a new widget. By clicking on 'Appearance', then 'Widgets', the list of available widgets appears which now includes 'GTranslate'. Dragging this widget to a sidebar or other area will make a new translation feature appear on the prototype site wherever widgets are displayed. For example, dragging the 'GTranslate' widget to the 'Footer 1' area of the standard 'Twenty Seventeen' theme will make the translation feature appear on the bottom of every page. Remember that each theme has its own unique areas for placing widgets and that not all areas appear on every page. For example, in the 'Twenty Seventeen' theme, the 'Blog Sidebar' area only appears when blog posts are displayed, but not on regular pages.

The 'GTranslate' plugin illustrates a few common steps in plugin installation. First, it requires some initial configuration, or setup. Other plugins with more features will have more complicated installation procedures. Second, plugins make new options available. This plugin made a new widget available but customers couldn't access that feature until the widget was activated in a sidebar, footer, or other screen area. New options created by a plugin may include some combination of:

- A new menu in the administrator area, either on its own or under 'Settings'.

- A new widget, or widgets, to be placed in sidebars and footers.

- A new content type, such as contact forms or maps. New content can be created and then added to the prototype site by placing it on pages or posts.

Plugins for Front-End Features

Tens of thousands of plugins are available at the official WordPress directory wordpress.org/plugins. As with themes, the best guarantee of quality is popularity, or number of downloads, followed by how recently the plugin was updated. Because plugins contain code, plugins have to be constantly updated to deal with security threats and WordPress software updates. Ratings and reviews can also be helpful for choosing plugins if there are enough comments to make a rating reliable. Because of WordPress' popularity, Internet searches will reveal much discussion online about the best plugins for particular needs. There are usually many plugins available for the same features, so if one plugin isn't meeting your needs, move on to the next.

There are three kinds of plugins, each of which behaves differently and adds different kinds of features. Plugins can add *front-end features* that customers interact with, such as a contact form or the translation feature discussed earlier. Plugins can add *back-end features* that work behind the scenes, such as changing the administrative area or providing additional security, but don't change the appearance of a site or its content. Plugins can also add *integration features* that connect a prototype site to other Internet services, such as live updates of an Instagram feed or a Google map.

As in the 'GTranslate' plugin example, front-end features normally require initial configuration, then afterwards the selection of additional options to make the feature appear on the site. Another example of a front-end feature plugin is adding a contact form. Contact forms are useful for many different kinds of customer interactions from product and service requests to feedback on the prototype itself.

There are many different contact form plugins to choose from. For this example, we will install 'Ninja Forms', one of the easier contact form plugins to use. From the WordPress administrator area, select 'Plugins' on the left, then 'Add New', then type 'Ninja Forms' in the search box on the upper right. Install and activate the 'Ninja Forms' plugin.

'Ninja Forms' is an example of a plugin that creates a new content type, a form, in addition to the standard WordPress content types of pages and posts. Each content type has its own unique format and is displayed in its own unique way. To start using the plugin, a new contact form has to be created, then the contact form needs to be placed somewhere on the prototype site.

After installing 'Ninja Forms', a new menu called 'Ninja Forms' will appear on the upper left of the administrator area, just under pages and posts. Select the 'Ninja Forms' menu item, click on 'Add New', then choose the template called 'Contact Us'. This creates a new form with four fields, or places that customers can enter information in specific formats. Clicking on the settings gear to the right of each field, such as 'Name' or 'Email', allows changes to be made to each field. The '+' button on the lower right allows new fields to be added, and fields can be rearranged by clicking and dragging. Save the form by clicking 'PUBLISH' in the upper right, then leaving the edit screen by clicking on the 'x' in the upper right corner.

The Ninja Forms dashboard should list your new form. A prototype site can have more than one form, depending on what information needs to be collected from a customer. For a form to be visible to a customer, it needs to be added to a page or post. When editing a page or post, a new button called 'Add Form' has been added next to the 'Add Media' button near the top of the editor.

Another option is to copy and paste a *shortcode* into a page or post. The Ninja Forms dashboard lists each of the forms created along with their shortcode, which should look something like '[ninja_form id=1]'. WordPress will automatically convert the shortcode into the form. Ninja Forms also adds a new widget, which can be used to place a form in a sidebar, footer, or other screen area defined by a theme.

Plugins for Back-End Features

Back-end features work behind the scenes of a prototype site, making the site perform better, more secure, or easier to edit and administer. An example of a new back-end feature would be a visual overview of all pages that allows dragging and dropping to rearrange pages—extra features for a site administrator that are lacking in the standard WordPress 'All Pages' display under the 'Pages' menu. From the WordPress administrator area, select 'Plugins', then 'Add New'. Type 'cms tree page view' into the search box on the upper right. One of the first results should be the 'CMS Tree Page View' plugin. Install and activate this plugin.

Once activated, a new menu option for a 'Tree View' will be available under the 'Pages' on the left of the screen. This new view allows pages to be rearranged and added by dragging and clicking. Many back-end features are designed to make life as a prototype builder and site administrator a little bit easier.

Other important types of back-end features include:

Increased security—a fact of life on the Internet is being vulnerable to break-in attempts. Security plugins take additional steps to harden a prototype site and monitor attempts to break in. The 'Wordfence' plugin is a popular choice for a security plugin. Once you see how many attempts are made to break into a site every day, you will be motivated to further improve your security. More about security will be discussed in Chapter 13.

Faster performance—using software such as WordPress to generate web pages is effective in many ways, but speed can be a disadvantage. Compared to delivering static web pages to customers, WordPress pages can be slow to load in a browser, particularly when using inexpensive shared web hosting. There are many ways to improve site speed which will be discussed in Chapter 13, but an easy remedy is to use a cache (pronounced like CASH) plugin. A cache will save copies of commonly requested web pages and send out copies without having to run code and recreate them every time. The 'WP Super Cache' plugin is currently a good choice for a cache plugin.

Backup and recovery—there are few worse things for digital entrepreneurs than having an important site go down. There is no such thing as error-free software or hardware (or humans), so having a recent backup of a site is critical, as well as the ability to recover from a problem by getting a backup copy of a site up and running again. A number of backup plugins such as 'Updraft Plus' can be configured to do automatic backups and can recover a saved site with a few clicks. Practicing recovery from a backup before it happens is critical.

Plugins for back-end features may improve your prototype without much configuration, but each of these plugins has a complex set of configuration options to master in order to use them fully. Digital entrepreneurs need to make smart tradeoffs between the simplicity of the prototype and the need to add features that will help users discover the right product and service. Each plugin added to a prototype is an additional set of code that has to be learned, updated, and managed.

Plugins for Integration Features

One of the most powerful aspects of digital technology in the Internet era is the ability to combine and build upon the work of others. There is no need for digital entrepreneurs to reinvent technology for maps, status updates, or photo sharing when these services are available to use on their prototype sites. Features such as live Twitter or Instagram feeds are called integration features because they require integration, or a working connection, with an outside service. Integration features normally require setting up an account on the service provider, and sometimes require obtaining a unique identifier or API key that verifies your right to use a service.

An example of an integration feature typically used by a business prototype is a Google map. To use a Google map plugin, a unique identifier called an API key must be created from a Google account. From the WordPress administrator area, select 'Plugins', then 'Add New'. Search for 'google maps widget' in the upper right. One of the first results should be 'Google Maps Widget— Ultimate Google Maps Plugin'. Install and activate this plugin.

As part of the initial configuration, a Google Maps API Key needs to be created, then copied and pasted into the plugin. From the 'Settings' menu in the administrator area, select 'Google Maps Widget'. The plugin will have a link to instructions for creating a Google Maps API key. Follow the instructions, then copy and paste a very long API key into the 'Google Maps API Key' field. Go to the 'Appearance' menu, then 'Widgets', to add a Google Maps Widget to a screen area such as 'Footer 1' in the 'Twenty Seventeen' theme. Enter an address, save the changes, and look at the site to see if the map appears.

Fixing problems with integration features is doubly annoying because the problem could either be on your site or the outside service, or how they communicate with each other. Help forums are your first source of information for integration feature problems, but a change of plugin can also be a good strategy. There are many Google map plugins to choose from.

Social media is another common type of integration feature. Plugins make it easy to add feeds from social media, such as Facebook, Twitter, or Instagram. In each case, creating something similar to an API key is usually required. Integration features can do more than read information from an outside service. They can also be useful for automatically broadcasting content to other sites for promotion purposes, such as an automatic Tweet when a new post is published. Adding Facebook 'like' buttons can encourage customers to promote your content on their own news feeds. A plugin called 'Slack Notifications' will automatically send site updates to a Slack channel. Integration with outside services can be even deeper, such as a plugin for live chat that integrates with an outside customer support service, an example being the 'Zendesk Chat' plugin. The wide range of integration features available dramatically increases the power of business prototyping.

Useful Features for Content and Community Businesses

Adding new features via plugins is a great way to turn a generic web site into a more targeted prototype for a new business idea. There are new features available for each of the five basic types of digital business discussed in Chapter 2.

For content-based businesses, the most pressing problem is usually creating the content itself rather than adding many new features. Better editor plugins such as 'TinyMCE Advanced' make content creation and editing that much easier. For more control over how content appears, visual page builders have become popular for creating more elaborate layouts within pages and posts. 'Elementor' is a highly used page builder plugin.

A popular addition for content sites is a social sharing plugin that automatically add social media buttons to all content, making it easy for visitors to promote content in their own feeds. The 'AddToAny Share Buttons' is a popular choice, but there are many others. To keep visitors engaged, it's useful to recommend other popular or related content on site to encourage them to read more. 'WordPress Popular Posts' is a plugin that makes visible the most popular content on site, while the multi-featured 'Jetpack' plugin includes a related posts widget.

Content-based businesses often try advertising as a revenue model. One of the largest advertising networks for small publishers is Google AdSense. After signing up and being approved for an AdSense account, advertisements can be added to a web page by cutting and pasting HTML code. Plugins such as 'Ad Inserter' make inserting AdSense into WordPress sites easier.

For community-based businesses, even a basic WordPress site offers the opportunity for people to comment on any page or post and respond to those comments. To create a more fully featured forum or discussion board, a discussion plugin such as 'bbPress' can be added. Other specialized types of community can be created with plugins for business directory and review sites, such as the 'Business Directory Plugin' which creates a Yelp-like review site.

A simpler option for reviews is to use a plugin such as 'WP Product Review Lite', which allows the content of any post to be reviewed. To create a fully featured social media site, complete with profiles, friending, and news feeds, 'BuddyPress' is the plugin of choice. Installing and configuring BuddyPress is complex because of its many features, so trying it first on a separate test site is recommended before committing to it on a business prototype.

Useful Features for Online Stores

A very simple online store can be created with a payment button. With a PayPal Business account, simple 'Buy Now' buttons can be created from the 'Tools' page at the PayPal site. Button code can be copied and pasted on to a page or post. A plugin such as 'PayPal Buy Now Button' will do the same job. Place the 'Buy Now' button near a description of your product or service, and you are ready to receive payments.

A payment button is fine for selling only a single product, or even a few, but as soon as customers might want to find and buy multiple items in a single transaction a shopping cart is needed. A shopping cart feature allows customers to put items in and out of a cart and check out with multiple payment and shipping options.

The 'WooCommerce' plugin has become the most popular way to turn a WordPress site into a full online store. In addition to the base 'WooCommerce' plugin, there are dozens of additional plugins to add new payment methods, new shipping methods, and many other features to WooCommerce sites. As with BuddyPress, WooCommerce is a complex plugin that makes extensive changes to a site, so it is best to experiment with a test site first to see if WooCommerce is right for your prototype. Setup and configuration of a WooCommerce site takes some reading of instructions, which not all digital entrepreneurs enjoy.

Live customer service and support can be a powerful way of increasing online sales. A chat feature that integrates with another chat service, such as the 'Zendesk Chat' plugin mentioned earlier, can be useful for online stores, as can a stand-alone chat feature such as the plugin 'WP Live Chat Support'.

Another option for online stores is to use an outside paid service, such as Shopify, to host the actual store and complete sales transactions. The prototype site could either feature Shopify 'Buy Now' buttons, along with additional content, discussion, or customer features, or integrate with Shopify using a plugin such as 'WP Shopify'.

Useful Features for Matchmaker Businesses

A matchmaker-based business is more challenging to implement in general purpose content management software like WordPress. Simple matchmaking can be done by manually entering information about potential matches on pages or posts, then allowing customers to express interest via comments or contact forms. As the number of users grows, however, a matchmaking business will want to allow people to automatically sign up and post information about potential matches. Matchmaking sites at a larger scale also want to complete transactions on site easily and provide sophisticated searching capabilities.

There is no one WordPress plugin that covers all these desirable matchmaking features. A membership plugin such as 'Ultimate Member' is a popular choice for letting customers sign up on their own and adding customized information to their profiles. A social login plugin such as 'Nextend Social Login and Register' can encourage membership by not burdening customers with the need to set up another yet another account and password. If matchmaking will be restricted to paid customers, a plugin such as 'Simple Membership' will allow only paid customers to access specific site content.

A different possibility for a more self-service matchmaking approach is to repurpose a classified ads feature. A plugin such as 'WPAdverts' will turn a prototype into a classified ad site, allowing buyers and sellers to perform transactions with each other and provide the option of charging customers for posting ads.

Useful Features for Promoting an Existing Business

Content management software like WordPress is effective for promoting an existing business, particularly small businesses, even without additional features. Adding and editing content is easy, which is the number one challenge for small business sites. A typical business promotion site may not need much in the way of additional features. In the same way that business themes should lean toward a minimalist look at the beginning, in order to keep customers focused on the most important messages and not be confused, an argument can be made that adding lots of additional features might distract from a clear brand message [4]. Clear content, high quality images, easy to understand menus, and a prominent search function are the first priorities for business promotion sites.

It can be useful to add standard small business features to a prototype site. Typical features include contact forms as discussed earlier, a Google map for business location, displaying business hours in a standard format (using a plugin such as 'Business Hours Indicator'), collecting and displaying customer testimonials (using the 'Strong Testimonials' plugin), and showing a Frequently Asked Questions list (using the 'Arconix FAQ' or similar plugin).

For business promotion, one of the most powerful methods of attracting and engaging new customers is to build a list of email addresses and communicate with subscribers via regular newsletters. Because of spam filters and other limitations on how many emails can be sent by a web hosting service, typically an outside email marketing service is used together with a WordPress plugin that integrates with the outside service. MailChimp is a popular choice because it is free to use for the first few thousand email addresses. The official MailChimp integration plugin 'MailChimp for WordPress' is widely used in the WordPress community. More about email marketing will be discussed in Chapter 11.

In this chapter, we have barely scraped the surface of the tens of thousands of freely available WordPress plugins, not to mention the many professional plugins that are for sale. By all means, try adding lots of different features to your business prototypes if you feel they might make a real difference to your digital business. But remember that oftentimes less is more with a business prototype. Don't add new features to an MVP that will confuse potential customers. Don't overcommit to using a complicated feature before you figure out customer needs. And don't use fancy plugins as an excuse to delay contact with potential customers. If billion-dollar startup unicorns like Zappos and Groupon started as no more than basic blogs, what are you waiting for?

Additional Resources

https://wordpress.org/plugins/gtranslate/—language translation using Google Translate.

https://wordpress.org/plugins/ninja-forms/—easy to use contact forms.

https://wordpress.org/plugins/tinymce-advanced/—more powerful page and post editor.

https://wordpress.org/plugins/wordfence/—advanced security plugin.

https://wordpress.org/plugins/wp-super-cache/—caching plugin to speed up site loading times.

https://wordpress.org/plugins/updraftplus/—easy to use site backup and recovery.

https://wordpress.org/plugins/google-maps-widget/—Google map widgets.

https://wordpress.org/plugins/dorzki-notifications-to-slack/—site updates broadcast to a Slack channel.

https://wordpress.org/plugins/zopim-live-chat/—add live chat using Zendesk.

https://wordpress.org/plugins/elementor/—visual page builder for editing complex page layouts.

https://wordpress.org/plugins/add-to-any/—add social media share buttons to any content.

https://wordpress.org/plugins/wordpress-popular-posts/—display the most popular posts.

https://wordpress.org/plugins/jetpack/—integration with the
wordpress.com service that includes many features,
including a related posts widget.

https://wordpress.org/plugins/ad-inserter/—publish
advertisements from the Google AdSense network.

https://wordpress.org/plugins/business-directory-plugin/—
create a business directory and review site.

https://wordpress.org/plugins/wp-product-review/—add
review capability to any post.

https://wordpress.org/plugins/buddypress/—create a full
featured social media site.

https://wordpress.org/plugins/wp-ecommerce-paypal/—
display a PayPal Buy Now button.

https://wordpress.org/plugins/woocommerce/—create an
online store with shopping cart.

https://wordpress.org/plugins/wp-live-chat-support/—add
a live chat feature.

https://wordpress.org/plugins/wpshopify/—connect a site
with a Shopify online store.

https://wordpress.org/plugins/ultimate-member/—allow site
members to create full profiles.

https://wordpress.org/plugins/nextend-facebook-connect/—
allow members to log in using their existing social media
accounts.

https://wordpress.org/plugins/simple-membership/—allow
content to be restricted based on paid membership.

https://wordpress.org/plugins/business-hours-indicator/—
display opening hours for a business.

https://wordpress.org/plugins/arconix-faq/—add a frequently
asked question list.

https://wordpress.org/plugins/mailchimp-for-wp/—
collect email addresses and use MailChimp to send
newsletters.

Exercises

7.1. Install and configure a translation plugin, a contact
form plugin, and an improved visual editor plugin on
your prototype site.

7.2. Install and configure a Google Map plugin on your prototype site, making sure your Google Maps API key works correctly.

7.3. Choose three plugins that are appropriate for your type of digital business. Discuss what business benefits are likely to result from each of their features. Install and configure these plugins on your prototype site.

References

[1]   Rocket Media. *Static Vs. Dynamic Websites: What Are They and Which Is Better?* (2013), available: https://rocketmedia.com/blog/static-vs-dynamic-websites. [Accessed: July 14, 2018].

[2]   D. Pataki. *Learning Php for Wordpress Development: A Comprehensive Guide.* (2017), available: https://premium.wpmudev.org/blog/getting-started-with-wordpress-development/. [Accessed: July 20, 2018].

[3]   R. McCollin. *Javascript for Wordpress People: What You Need to Know.* (2016), available: https://premium.wpmudev.org/blog/javascript-for-wordpress-people/. [Accessed: July 21, 2018].

[4]   K. Krol, *Wordpress Complete.* Birmingham, UK: Packt Publishing Ltd, 2017.

Web Analytics

Highlights

Chapter 8 introduces web analytics and the data it makes available about business prototype performance.

- Digital businesses use web analytics to learn more about how potential customers are using a web site.

- Web analytics provides data on all three phases of the ABC process: how many potential customers are acquired through each online channel; how visitors behave on a prototype; and the conversion actions taken by visitors that reflect business success. Web analytics also relates these phases to each other by, for example, showing which online channels result in the most successful conversions.

- Web analytics tracks visitor actions through information that is collected every time a web page loads in a browser and by collecting information about specific on-page actions.

- Web analytics reporting and measurement depend on assumptions that may or may not be appropriate for a particular digital business.

- By the end of the chapter, the reader should be able to install web analytics tracking on a prototype and test that web analytics is working properly.

How Web Analytics Works

Web analytics is a technology that measures the performance of web sites, including digital business prototypes. Web analytics provides data on all three steps of the ABC process, including how many visitors have been acquired, user behavior, and the actions taken by customers that lead to business results. Web analytics provides the data to answer important business questions such as:

- How many visitors came to our site?

- How did they get here? Did they search for us, click on an advertisement, or follow a link from another site?

- Which pages are the most popular?

- How many visitors watched an introductory video?

- How often did visitors look at the help pages?

Even though web analytics technology is quite widespread in business practice, there's very little academic research about it. Without analytics data, the whole entrepreneurial model of digital prototyping and business experimentation becomes difficult, if not impossible. Early research suggests that marketing efforts especially benefit from having detailed information about the effectiveness of campaigns and marketing efforts, and that businesses with complex or lengthy sales processes also benefit greatly from more detailed data about customer journeys and user experiences [1].

The most widely used web analytics service, Google Analytics (GA), is part of the Google Marketing Platform. Over 85% of all sites that use web analytics, or 55% of all web sites, subscribe to Google Analytics [2]. GA is free to use at the basic level. GA dominates the web analytics world, but other analytics services work similarly.

Web analytics collects data on visitors by adding tracking code to each web page and by saving small history files called *cookies* in a visitor's web browser. The tracking code sends a message to the GA service every time a web page is loaded into a browser. This message records an interaction called a *pageview* in GA, and it includes:

- The URL and title of the page being viewed.

- The IP address of the client that asked for the page and the domain name previously visited.

- The technology being used to view the page (screen size, device, platform, etc.).

- Time and date.

- Data stored in a cookie about previous visits, if a cookie exists.

By recording a series of pageviews, Google Analytics can tell entrepreneurs quite a lot about what's happening on their business prototypes. The URLs and titles tell us which pages are visited the most and in what sequence. IP addresses and previously visited domain names tell us where a visitor is located (within certain limits) and which sites are the sources of potential customers. The technology information can tell us if the site is more or less popular with certain platforms (for example, Android vs. Apple) or devices (laptops vs. phones). The time and date of a series of pageviews can tell us how long a visitor stays on site, and which content visitors spend more time on. Data stored in cookies can tell us whether a visitor is new to our site or if they are a returning visitor.

The standard pageview tracking code, written in Javascript, is added to the HTML code of a web page in the <head> section. If a site uses content management software such as WordPress, a plugin can be used to automatically insert the tracking code on every page. The web analytics tracking code is unique to your web site.

In addition to the pageview tracking code, additional pieces of tracking code can be added to other HTML tags on your site. This code sends messages about additional interactions called *events* in Google Analytics. Events are other interactions on a web site that don't involve loading a new web page into a browser.

Depending on your business idea, examples of important events to track might include:

- Clicking on a link to another site, or an *outbound link*.

- Downloading a document.

- Clicking on an email link.

- Clicking on a button to submit a form.

- Playing a video.

- Starting a live chat.

- Scrolling to, or hovering over, a part of the screen.

For example, to add event tracking code to an outbound link like this:

```
<a href="www.jpedia.org">Link to an
external site.</a>
```

the additional event tracking code might look something like this:

```
<a href="www.jpedia.org" onclick=
"ga('send', 'event', 'CATEGORY', 'ACTION',
'LABEL');">Link to an external site.</a>
```

where 'CATEGORY', 'ACTION', and 'LABEL' are filled in with labels of your own choice for tracking purposes. Typically, 'CATEGORY' would be set to the type of interaction, such as 'outbound-link' or 'external-link', while 'ACTION' and 'LABEL' would be more specific information, such as the domain name and exact URL. 'CATEGORY' and 'ACTION' are required, while 'LABEL' is optional. The 'onclick' is one kind of HTML document event, a button click, that Javascript can track, but there are many others such as a key press on a keyboard or hovering over a link.

Event tracking can be added directly to HTML code, or plugins are available that will automatically track certain kinds of events such as outbound links and downloads. Pageviews and events can only be tracked on your own sites, because your unique tracking code is not placed on web pages on sites that are controlled by others. Pageviews on other sites cannot be seen by you, which is why the final click on a link that takes a visitor to another site can only be tracked as an event.

For Google Analytics to work, the correct tracking code needs to be placed on each web page to record pageviews, with additional tracking code as needed to record events. A web browser must have Javascript and cookies enabled for tracking to work properly. Fortunately, only about 1% of visitors completely disable one or both of these [3], but up to 30% might erase their cookies at least once a month. Privacy is an increasingly important issue and some browsers are choosing to block web analytics tracking either by default or with the use of browser add-ons. Web analytics data, as revealing and powerful as it is, always needs to be interpreted with caution.

Web Analytics Measures

Google Analytics captures the raw data from the two kinds of user interactions, pageviews and events, and creates a number of useful measures of web site performance, including:

Sessions—a session, sometimes called a visit, is a series of interactions within a certain time period. By default, interactions tracked by Google Analytics within a 30-minute time period are counted as one session, but the maximum length of a session can be changed. A series of pageviews and events longer than 30 minutes will count as more than one session.

Users, New and Returning—Google Analytics creates a unique user ID for every visit, which identifies a sequence of pageviews and events as coming from a single user. If a browser allows GA cookies to be stored, the same user ID can be used in the next session and the visitor can be recognized as a returning user rather than a new user. By default, Google Analytics does not recognize the same user across different web browsers and devices, though additional coding can keep track of this information.

Active Users—the number of users currently interacting with a site. Active users are visible in the 'Real Time' reports in Google Analytics, while most other data is delayed by up to 24 hours.

Bounce Rate—a session that has no interactions after the first pageview is called a *bounce*. The bounce rate is the percentage of all sessions that are bounces. Because a bounce, where a user arrives at a site and immediately leaves, is considered a failure for many digital businesses, bounce rate is one of the most immediate measures of site performance.

Session Duration—the length of time between the first and last interaction in a session. Longer session durations might be considered a positive in a content-based business, suggesting that visitors find the content more engaging. In a more transaction-oriented business, however, longer times might reflect confusion about how to navigate a site. Session duration also doesn't tell us whether a user read our content for 15 minutes, or if they stepped out for a cup of coffee for 15 minutes and clicked away later.

Traffic Medium, Source, and Channel—each session is assigned a medium and a source to describe where a user came from. The medium is the most generic description of traffic sources. Possible medium values include *referrals* (the visitor followed a link from another web site); *organic* (the visitor came from the unpaid or 'organic' results of a search); *paidsearch* (the visitor came from advertisements on search results); or *none* (the visitor came some other way, including typing a domain name directly into a browser). The source is the name of the specific site, if any, that a visit came from. Common combinations of medium and source are grouped into channels which provide a generic set of traffic sources that is more specific than a medium.

Entrances and Exits—the first and last pages visited in a session. Different entrances can be used to test whether a particular campaign, such as a set of Twitter tweets, is more effective at generating traffic and acquiring customers than a set of Facebook status updates which link to a different entrance page. Exit pages are sometimes used to determine which parts of a site are more likely to drive visitors away.

Location—by recording the IP addresses of visitors, Google Analytics can guess where a visitor is located, by city and country. IP addresses are usually unique to Internet Service Providers rather than individuals, so location information is often useful enough but not perfect.

Device—Google Analytics receives information about the browser being used, which language it is set to, which platform or operating system is running on a device, and the current size of the screen. With this information, GA can usually determine, for example, which visitors are using an Android phone versus a Windows laptop.

Demographics and Interests—beyond the IP address and the history of interactions on your site, Google Analytics has little information about a visitor. The larger Google advertising network and other major ad networks often have much more information about a person. By visiting adssettings.google.com, you can see the demographic information and set of interests that Google associates with you as an individual, along with a detailed stream of activity across web sites and mobile apps. This information, available for visitors to a site who are logged into Google, can be accessed in analytics by turning on the Demographics and Interests option in GA.

Goals and Conversions—any interaction, including pageviews and events, can be defined as a goal. A goal represents a session that has a successful business outcome, whether it be buying something, contacting a business, or clicking on an advertisement. A conversion is recorded when a visitor successfully reaches a goal. Goals and conversions will be discussed in detail in Chapter 9.

The meaning of the raw interactions data, the pageviews and events, is fairly straightforward, given an understanding of how pageviews are recorded and by knowing that events are only tracked if code is specifically added to track them. Other measures derived from pageviews and events, however, are calculated based on additional assumptions and might require more careful interpretation. For example, session times may not include the time spent on the last page visited because a click on an outbound link to leave a site is not recorded as a pageview. Sometimes it is more useful to look at trends, which show improvement or decline, rather than treat the values themselves as completely accurate. Returning users are usually underreported, because not every person will always use the same browser or device to access your site and not every browser will allow cookies to be stored.

Because web analytics provides performance information at such an incredible level of detail, it is easy to convince ourselves that we are being presented with 'the truth'. It is a skill to turn analytics data into actionable insight—answering the 'what should we do?' question is something that digital entrepreneurs can learn with practice. Translating between web analytics measures and the Key Performance Indicators (KPIs) that businesses use to evaluate their performance still requires some work.

Web Analytics Reports

Analytics reports provide data about measures of digital business performance over time, but also allow entrepreneurs to ask important business questions by combining and comparing different measures. The main reports in Google Analytics are structured around the ABC process: audience and acquisition, behavior, and conversions.

Audience—reporting about numbers of visitors, how often they return, where they come from, and what technology they use. If an GA account is linked to a Google advertising account, information is available about visitor age, gender, and interests. These reports can be used to, for example, identify new countries or areas that are unexpectedly interested in a digital business and tailor more content, products, or services for those regions. Audience reports can also reveal how often users return to a business and how many visits it takes a typical visitor to convert. The technology used can reveal whether a site needs to be better customized for a particular device or browser.

Acquisition—reporting about the medium, source, and channels sending visitors to a site. Finding the best sources of new customers is hugely important for digital businesses. By integrating Google Analytics with other services more detailed acquisition information is available. For example, by combining GA with a Google Ads account the analytics reports will contain detailed information about which advertisements and keywords were more successful for customer acquisition. By linking up with a Google Search Console account, the analytics reports will include the exact search phrases that visitors use to find your business.

Customer acquisition reporting can be made even more precise by defining *campaigns*. A campaign is a specific set of marketing activities intended to generate new customer leads, such as an advertising campaign or a series of local events. Each campaign can be given a unique URL for clicking to a prototype site by adding additional parameters at the end of the URL. Acquisition reports can then be used to figure out which campaigns were more effective, even if they came from the same source.

Behavior—reporting about how often pageviews and events are recorded and in what sequence. Behavior reports show the most popular content, information that can be used to adjust how articles, product descriptions, and blog posts are written in the future. Behavior flow reports can be used to look for unexpected paths that customers take through a site. For example, does looking at a page with deals or discounts lead visitors next to a product information page or a purchase page? Are there pathways that unexpectedly cause visitors to exit a site? Behavior reports also report on page loading times, which can be used to identify slow pages that might be frustrating potential customers.

Behavior reports can also be linked to other Google services. By linking to a Google AdSense account, digital entrepreneurs can see which content on their site is generating more advertising revenue. Behavior reporting can show the results of experiments created in Google Optimize, where different versions of a page are randomly assigned to visitors to see which version performs better. Experiments and Google Optimize will be discussed in Chapter 12.

Conversions—reporting about how often visitors convert. A conversion is tracked either through a pageview or an event that is defined as a goal in Google Analytics. Because conversions reflect business success, tracing back successful conversions to behavior (which pages were visited) and acquisitions (where visitors came from) is where the power of web analytics truly lies. Constantly improving the process of acquiring customers and improving user experiences that lead to conversions is one of the most powerful advantages that digital entrepreneurs have. Conversion goals will be discussed in more detail in Chapter 9.

A consistent path to conversion by visiting a sequence of pages is called a *funnel*. For example, a shopping funnel could include a sequence of web pages for putting a product in a cart, entering shipping information, and then entering payment information. Conversion reports can show if specific steps in the funnel are losing customers.

Conversion reports can also use customer *segmentation* to improve performance reporting. Segments can be used to divide visitors into distinct groups with different objectives. For example, one group of visitors might be searching for information about a product versus another group that is ready to buy. Web site performance can be measured differently for each subgroup. If there is a large enough group of visitors whose actions are not as important, such as visitors who leave a site quickly, then focusing on the data for a segment of potential customers can be more insightful than reporting average measurements for the entire site.

For all reports, measures can be related to each other by adding new *dimensions* that cut across customer acquisition, behavior, and conversions data. One popular example is to add the source of customer acquisition as a dimension to a conversions report, answering the question of which visitors are more likely to lead to business success. Analytics reports can also compare results to site averages, for example showing which pages have higher or lower bounce rates than average. Or, by agreeing to share data with others, Google Analytics can benchmark performance against other similar sites.

Setting Up and Configuring Web Analytics

Setting up Google Analytics is free and easy. A new GA account can be set up by visiting marketingplatform. google.com/about/analytics and logging in with a Google username and password. (Some Google accounts administered by schools have Google Analytics capabilities turned off. If so, create a new Gmail or other Google account and use the new account to log in.) Select a 'Website' for tracking and enter an account name.

Each GA account can have up to 50 *properties*. Each property corresponds to a different web site, located at its own URL. Enter a name and the URL of the prototype site to be tracked by Google Analytics. Click on the 'Get Tracking ID' button at the bottom. This will create a unique tracking ID for your site and make available the tracking code for your site.

Each property in GA has at least one *view*. All new properties start with one view, called 'All Web Site Data'. Additional views can be created to share subsets of web site data with specific users. For example, a new view limited to data from United States visitors could be created and shared with an employee or contractor only responsible for American customers. Users can be added to an entire GA account, a specific web site property, or only to a specific view by selecting 'User Management' from the 'ADMIN' menu of the Google Analytics account and adding a new user's email address.

The tracking code provided by GA can be copied and pasted into every web page to be tracked. If your prototype site uses content management software, such as WordPress, then plugins are available that will automatically add the correct tracking code to each page on your site. To do this, install the plugin 'Google Analytics Dashboard for WP' on your WordPress site and activate. A new menu called 'Google Analytics' will appear on the left of the WordPress administrator area. Select this menu and click on the 'Authorize Plugin' button. Follow the instructions to obtain an access code from Google. Select a view that includes your site URL, then 'Save Changes' at the bottom of the screen.

To confirm that Google Analytics is successfully tracking interactions on your site, return to your Google Analytics account and select 'REAL-TIME' from the reports menu on the left side of the screen, then 'Overview'. Load a page from your site into another tab on a web browser. If GA shows an active user on your site, congratulations, Google Analytics is working! Real Time reports should show results immediately, but it can take up to 24 hours for data to appear in the other standard reports.

When first installed, the Google Analytics plugin is only tracking pageviews, but not events. To turn on event tracking, go to the 'Google Analytics' menu in your WordPress administrative area, select 'Tracking Code', then the 'Events Tracking' tab. Turn on any events you wish to track such as downloads and outbound links, and click 'Save Changes' at the bottom. You can confirm that events are being tracked by adding an outbound link on your prototype site, clicking on the outbound link, then looking at the 'REAL-TIME' 'Events' report in Google Analytics.

Once Google Analytics is proven to be working it's common practice to stop tracking your own visits to your site. By selecting the 'Exclude Tracking' tab, then clicking on the 'Administrator' check box and saving, the plugin will ignore your own visits and track only your potential customers instead.

Google Analytics works well on its own, but it can also be used together with the Google Tag Manager. Instead of adding the GA tracking code directly to web pages, Google Tag Manager puts an empty container on every web page that can be filled with Google Analytics code or other types of code and rules, as specified in a Google Tag Manager account. Tag managers are most useful for people like marketers who want to be able to control what is tracked on a page but don't have access to the code themselves. Since we have control over our own sites, using a tag manager isn't required, but it is how more businesses will be managing Google Analytics code on their sites in the future.

Web analytics is an incredibly powerful tool for measuring the performance of web sites, and therefore for testing new digital business ideas. Once web analytics is installed and working, the real work of business experimentation can begin.

Additional Resources

www.w3schools.com/js/js_events_examples.asp—examples of other Javascript events that can trigger a Google Analytics event.

https://adssettings.google.com/—see the information that Google advertising networks have about yourself.

https://ads.google.com—Google Ads, one of the most popular services for designing and purchasing advertisements that will appear on other sites and appear on Google search results.

https://search.google.com/search-console—service for monitoring the use and health of websites, particularly useful for tracking the search terms that visitors enter to find a site.

https://ga-dev-tools.appspot.com/campaign-url-builder/— tool for creating URLs that add Google Analytics campaign information to a link.

www.google.com/adsense—Google AdSense, one of the largest services for publishing advertisements on a site.

https://marketingplatform.google.com/about/optimize/—Google Optimize, a service for performing content experiments.

https://marketingplatform.google.com/about/analytics/—sign up for Google Analytics here.

https://wordpress.org/plugins/google-analytics-dashboard-for-wp/—popular WordPress plugin for Google Analytics.

https://analytics.google.com/analytics/academy/—help and tutorial information about Google Analytics.

www.lunametrics.com/about-us/case-studies/—collection of Google Analytics-oriented success stories.

Exercises

8.1. List three important questions that web analytics can answer about your digital business prototype. Mention any specific measures that are most relevant.

8.2. Discuss whether any of the assumptions Google Analytics makes about your users and their technology will be of concern for your prototype. For example, will your users accept cookies? Will Javascript be activated in their browsers?

8.3. Create a Google Analytics account. Find the tracking ID for the GA property that will be used to track your digital business prototype.

8.4. Create a new view of your prototype's property in Google Analytics and give another user access to that view.

8.5. Connect Google Analytics to your prototype site. Using real time reports, show that the connection is working.

References

[1]   J. Järvinen and H. Karjaluoto, "The Use of Web
        Analytics for Digital Marketing Performance
        Measurement," *Industrial Marketing Management*,
        vol. 50, pp. 117–127, 2015.

[2]   w3techs.com. *Usage Statistics and Market Share
        of Google Analytics for Websites, July 2018*. (2018),
        available: www.w3techs.com/technologies/details/
        ta-googleanalytics/all/all. [Accessed: July 27, 2018].

[3]   F. Alhlou, S. Asif, and E. Fettman, *Google Analytics
        Breakthrough: From Zero to Business Impact*. Hoboken,
        NJ: John Wiley & Sons, 2016.

Creating and Tracking Business Goals

Highlights

Chapter 9 shows how to use web analytics technology to create and track business goals.

- Web analytics technology can be used to define and track business goals.

- Conversion goals are customer actions performed online that define business success. Examples of conversion goals include clicking on advertisements, filling in a contact form, or clicking to buy.

- By the end of this chapter, the reader should be able to implement typical conversion goals in web analytics.

- A second major milestone in digital entrepreneurship is the creation of a digital business prototype, connected to web analytics and with defined conversion goals, that is ready to be tested on potential customers. The prototype implements the digital business design from the first milestone and is a tool for testing that design.

What Are Conversion Goals?

Conversion goals are the specific customer activities performed on a site that define business success. Typical conversion goals include:

- Completing a purchase or donation.

- Clicking on an advertisement.

- Filling in and submitting a contact form.

- Requesting a coupon or discount code.

- Subscribing to a newsletter.

- Downloading a brochure, product information, menu, or white paper.

Ideally, conversion goals match as closely as possible to a customer activity that creates value, and provide evidence that a digital business prototype is leading to a successful new business. Receiving money from a customer is one obvious way to create value. But there can be other actions taken by visitors online that are valuable.

The more complex a product or service, the more likely that potential customers will need to perform other actions before a monetary transaction takes place. Customers might need more information about a product or service before they buy, or need to be persuaded to try a new product with a discount. For expensive services, such as legal assistance or consulting, potential customers usually need a conversation first to find out if the service is right for them. In these cases it is perfectly reasonable to have a conversion goal that doesn't generate revenue directly. Conversion goals such as a contact form completion or downloading product information can be important steps along the way to revenue generation.

In some cases, a conversion goal can be tied directly to a monetary value such as revenue per goal completion. For example, if a digital business can calculate from its data how many purchases are made by the average visitor that signs up for a newsletter and the average purchase amount, then it is easy to assign a value to each newsletter signup even though no money has been received directly.

Sometimes, digital businesses set more indirect engagement goals such as signups, content submissions, commenting, or sharing on social media. Engagement goals can be useful in the context of a larger marketing or brand awareness campaign. For a new business prototype, however, there is a risk of building a digital business that is very good at engaging people but not effective at converting them into customers. In the early stages of a business prototype, it is particularly important to test the ability to create customers, not only engagement. Make sure your engagement activities are creating value for the business.

How many conversion goals should a prototype have? For the best experimental results, ideally there should be a single conversion goal. A single goal keeps a business design focused. With one goal, interpreting web analytics data is much easier. It is easier to see if changes made to a prototype improve a business idea or make it worse. Google Analytics allows up to 20 conversion goals for each view, making it possible to use conversion goals as a way to track almost every meaningful visitor interaction. Our recommendation is to use conversion goals to focus only on the most important visitor actions for testing your business prototype.

Conversion Rates

The conversion rate is the percentage of sessions that result in a conversion goal. Conversion rates online are typically low. Rates are lowest for actions that are more demanding such as making a purchase, or that require more than a few seconds to complete. E-commerce merchants typically report 1–3% conversion rates for sales [1], with the top online retailers averaging 3.3%. Building a deeper relationship with customers can dramatically affect conversion rates. For example, visits from Amazon Prime subscribers convert to sales 74% of the time compared to 13% for non-Prime subscribers. Conversion goals that demand less of customers are likely to have higher conversion rates.

How can conversion rates be increased? The first page that visitors enter on a site, the *landing page*, is important [2]. Your entire digital business prototype can be thought of as a persuasion device to convince a customer to accept a value proposition and it starts with a focused landing page. The landing page should clearly describe the value proposition for customers—what's in it for them?—explaining how the perceived benefits of taking action online outweigh the perceived costs and risks. The value proposition should be relevant to the visitor, show benefits that are higher than the costs, and provide an obvious way of accepting the proposition—a clear *call to action*.

A good landing page matches or exceeds customer expectations. The landing page should not contain any content that is confusing, distracting, or creates anxiety [2]. According to Croxen-John and van Tonder, a good model for thinking about calls to action on a landing page is to consider that a behavior such as a conversion is induced by the combination of three things: a motivation, an ability to act, and a trigger that creates immediacy or urgency [3].

Because motivation and triggers depend on emotion as well as rational decision-making there has been much attention paid to emotion in the conversion process. Some experts go as far as to display factual data only in a support role on other pages and focus entirely on emotional appeals for the landing page. All of the techniques applied to TV infomercials sales—creating a sense of scarcity through limited time offers, presenting an offer as a 'bargain', offering 'social proof' that people like yourself are happy with a purchase, or presenting an 'expert opinion' endorsing a product or service—are regularly used for online conversions as well. These techniques may seem annoying or tacky but part of the reason they persist is because in some situations, they work.

Another technique for increasing conversion rates is to create a situation that taps into a customer's feelings of reciprocity, involvement, and commitment. Research suggests that receiving something for free makes a visitor feel more obligated to reciprocate and offer something to the business in return, even if it is only a signup or email address. Luring a visitor into performing any activity, such as an online quiz, increases their time investment and may make them more likely to perform a conversion action.

Building and demonstrating trust is another effective way to increase conversion rates. As a relatively unknown startup in a digital world filled with potentially fraudulent activity, how will visitors feel comfortable enough to give your business information or a payment? High quality, error free content builds confidence, as do customer testimonials and reviews. Logos and badges from associations, awards, and payment companies can also build trust. Sometimes there is no substitute for business policies such as warranties, money back guarantees, service levels, or promises to respond to requests within a fixed period of time [4].

Common problems with landing pages can chase potential customers away and reduce conversion rates [5]. These problems include:

- An unclear call to action.

- Too many action choices, visual distractions, or too much text.

- Poor images or broken links.

- Writing mistakes.

- Not keeping promises made during customer acquisition (the ad says 'FREE puppies!', your site doesn't deliver).

- Asking for too much information or a lengthy sign-up process.

- Lack of trust and credibility guarantees or a lack of privacy guarantees.

- Slow pages and downloads.

- Poor performance on a particular device or browser, such as a non-mobile site viewed on a phone.

Implementing Conversion Goals: Destination Goals

In order to track conversions, conversion goals must be implemented in web analytics. As discussed in Chapter 8, Google Analytics tracks two kinds of visitor interactions: pageviews and events. A pageview message is sent to

GA when a web page with GA tracking code is loaded into a browser. An event message is sent to GA about any other on-page interaction, such as a click, that is being tracked with additional code on a web page.

Any pageview or event can be designated as a conversion goal. An example of a pageview conversion goal is a confirmation page that a visitor sees after performing a transaction. An example of an event conversion goal is a click on an image that contains an advertisement for another site.

To create a conversion goal based on a pageview, you will create what is called a *destination goal* in Google Analytics. Go to the Google Analytics 'ADMIN' screen for your prototype site and click on 'Goals' in the right most column under 'View'. Click on '+ NEW GOAL' to create a new conversion goal. Give the goal a name and select 'Destination' as the goal type. Under 'Goal details', set the destination as a page on your site, either using the entire URL, or only the part of the URL after the domain name. For example, if there is a page on the jpedia. org site with the address, www.jpedia.org/about-us/, entering '/about-us/' would work. Save the conversion goal.

To verify that the conversion goal is being tracked, go to 'REAL-TIME' reports on the left side of the Google Analytics 'ADMIN' screen, then select 'Conversions'. Load the destination page into a browser tab and verify that the conversion appears on the real time report.

A pageview conversion goal is a better indication of success if a visitor arrives at a page only after successfully completing an action. Some WordPress plugins will send visitors to a particular page after successfully completing an action such as a contact form submission or a user registration. This is known as a *redirect*.

To use redirects as a way to track successful completion of a contact form, for example, log into the administrator area of a WordPress site. Select 'Pages', then 'Add New' on the left-hand side. Create a page with the title 'Thank You', enter whatever text you like, and click on 'Publish' on the right. Copy the URL of the page. Using the 'Ninja Forms' plugin installed in Chapter 5, select 'Ninja Forms' on the left side of the WordPress administrator area, then select one of the contact forms already created. From the 'Emails & Actions' tab, turn on 'Redirect' and select the action gear on the right of the 'Redirect' row. Paste the URL of the 'Thank You' page into the 'URL' box, then click 'DONE', then 'PUBLISH'. Now, after this form is successfully submitted, the visitor will be taken to the 'Thank You' page. The URL for the 'Thank You' page can be used as a destination goal as described in the earlier example.

Redirects can be used to track other successful actions besides form completion. WordPress plugins exist that redirect after a registration, a login, or a logout. The most popular online store for WordPress sites, WooCommerce, has additional plugins that will redirect a customer to a confirmation page after successfully completing a purchase. Social button plugins allow for redirects after logging in to a site via Facebook or another social platform. PayPal payment buttons include a capability to redirect after completing a purchase.

Be sure not to place a link to a thank you or confirmation page on any menu or page that visitors would normally see. If the confirmation page for a purchase includes a unique ID number at the end of the URL, then each destination goal will have a slightly different URL. In these cases, use the 'Goal Details' in the GA view to set the URL of a goal to 'Begins With' rather than 'Equals To', and enter only the first part of the URL that stays the same for every purchase.

A destination goal can also define a funnel, or a series of pages visited in exact order on the way to a conversion goal. This is normally used in the context of a shopping cart where products are added to a cart, information is entered, and a purchase is completed. A funnel report will show where along the process visitors tend to exit, giving the entrepreneur valuable clues about where changes to their prototype site are needed.

Implementing Conversion Goals: Event Goals

Creating a conversion goal based on an event first requires that the appropriate Google Analytics code is added to a web page for that specific event. Event tracking code can be added directly to HTML on a web page, as shown in Chapter 8. For prototype builders using WordPress, however, it is usually easier to use plugins.

The easiest way to track event goals is when a Google Analytics plugin automatically adds the correct event tracking code. For example, the plugin used in Chapter 8, 'Google Analytics Dashboard for WP', will automatically add tracking code for common events such as outbound links and downloads.

From the 'Google Analytics' menu on the left of the WordPress administrator area, select 'Tracking Code', then the 'Events Tracking' tab. Turn on download and outbound link tracking, then click 'Save Changes' on the bottom of the screen. Add an outbound link to a page on your WordPress site, then load the page into a browser tab. Click on the outbound link, then look at the Google Analytics 'REAL-TIME' report for 'Events'. You should see an event in the report with an event category of 'outbound' and an event action of 'click'. Click on the 'outbound' event category link to see the event label, which is equal to the URL of the outbound link. Copy the URL in the label.

To define this event as a conversion goal, return to the Google Analytics 'ADMIN' page, select 'Goals' in the right column under 'View', and click on the '+ NEW GOAL' button. Give the goal a name, set the goal type to 'Event', and click 'Continue'. In 'Goal details', under 'Event conditions', enter the URL of the outbound link as equal to the 'Label' by pasting the URL. Save the goal. To test that event tracking is working, load the page with the outbound link in a browser tab, and click on the outbound link. Look at the real time 'Conversions' report in Google Analytics, where you should see a conversion.

There are two other options for tracking events that are not automatically generated by a WordPress GA plugin. First, a plugin called 'WP Google Analytics Events' can generate an event when any web page element is clicked if you know its CSS class or id. The CSS class or id can sometimes be found by inspecting the source code in a browser. A CSS id can also be added to your own HTML code, as in this example where the id 'MyEvent' has been added to a standard HTML link:

```
<a id="MyEvent" href="www.usfca.
edu/">Link to the USF home page.</a>
```

Another great option for generating Google Analytics events is to use Google Tag Manager. Instead of adding GA tracking code to every page on a site, a site using a tag manager will add code for an empty *container* on every page. The container will be filled later with whatever code is specified by the tag manager. This code can include standard Google Analytics pageview tracking but also many other kinds of tracking, such as code to monitor advertisements clicks and YouTube video plays. Each piece of code is called a *tag* and each tag is activated under certain conditions or *triggers*.

To use Google Tag Manager, sign up for a free account at tagmanager.google.com. Create a container for your prototype site. The first tag to add should be a 'Google Analytics—Universal Analytics' tag, with a 'Track Type' of 'Page View' and the tracking ID of the Google Analytics property for your prototype site. The trigger for this tag should be 'All Pages/Page View', so that a pageview message will be sent every time this page is loaded into a browser. Return to your WordPress administrator area, select 'Google Analytics' on the left, then 'Tracking Code'. Under the 'Basic Settings' tab, change the 'Tracking Type' to 'Tag Manager', enter the container ID you created above, and 'Save Changes'.

So far, using only this one tag, Google Tag Manager is simply repeating the normal GA functionality of tracking all pageviews. By adding additional Google Analytics tags with different triggers, however, the Tag Manager can generate events for advertisement clicks, YouTube views, and other interesting on-page actions without needing to change the underlying code. Google Tag Manager is particularly useful for tracking elements that are added to a site using the <iframe> tag, such as a YouTube video embed. Because the content of an <iframe> is controlled by another site it is difficult to collect information about what customers do in an <iframe> any other way.

Whenever implementing a conversion goal, make sure any advertisement blocking extensions are turned off in the browser you use to test your tracking. If tracking is not working in one browser try loading the page in another browser or have another person load the page from their computer.

Conversion Goals for Different Types of Digital Business

For all digital businesses, two common revenue generating conversion goals are purchases and advertisements. Immediate purchases are more appropriate for simpler products and services. An online store made with a shopping cart plugin such as WooCommerce, can be integrated with the Ecommerce reporting in Google Analytics. Simpler purchase mechanisms such as PayPal buttons can be set to redirect to a 'thank you' page created by you, which can be used as a destination goal in Google Analytics.

Some purchases are more complex, so it may be more appropriate to track the *micro conversions*, or customer actions that move a visitor closer to a purchase [6]. A contact form submission or a newsletter signup can be tracked using a 'thank you' or confirmation page. Downloads of product information or brochures can be tracked as events using Google Analytics plugins.

Other interactions such as clicks to send emails, make a phone call, or ask for a live chat can be tracked as events. A coupon or a deal can be published on a page and tracked as a destination goal. In the earlier stages of a digital business test, these micro conversions are less demanding of customers and might be a better starting point for experiments than waiting for a sufficient number of completed purchases.

Advertisements as a conversion goal can be tested either with live advertisements or with practice advertisements. A practice ad can be a link or an image made by the entrepreneur that sends a customer either to another site, or to a page on their own site, without any compensation. Practice ads can be tracked either as outbound link events or a destination page on a prototype site.

An entrepreneur can also sign up for live advertisements or affiliate links. Google AdSense is the largest advertising network for small web sites. AdSense is a free sign up, but there is a manual approval process that can take some time and isn't always successful. The approval process is easier to pass if the prototype site already has a critical mass of content and a constant or growing stream of visitors.

Once AdSense is approved, pieces of advertising code can be copied and pasted on to a prototype site, or a plugin can be used to place the code automatically. AdSense ads can be tracked in Google Analytics by linking an AdSense account with a GA account. Google Tag Manager can also be used to create an AdSense tag and a trigger that fires on every advertisement click. GA reports can then be used to see, for example, which content pages generate the most advertising revenue. Affiliate links can usually be tracked as outbound link events.

For content-based businesses, content reads can be tracked as destination goals. Video views are more challenging to track, but Google Tag Manager can be used for tracking YouTube plays and can even report on how long a video is watched. Conversion goals based on content viewing should be treated with caution, however, to make sure they eventually lead to an advertising click or some other valuable action.

Community-based businesses can use registrations or user signups as a potential conversion goal. Many WordPress registration or signup plugins will redirect to a confirmation page after completion, which can be used as a destination goal. Content submissions or comments can be tracked in the same way. Plugins exist for automatic content uploads by users, or with an early prototype one could simply use comments or contact forms. As with content viewing conversion goals, pay attention to whether community building leads to other valuable business interactions.

For matchmaker businesses, user signups and registration can be a conversion goal, similar to community-based businesses. In the early days of prototype testing, creating profile and searching for matches might be more of a manual process implemented through submissions of contact forms. Once customer demand on all sides is better understood, then additional technology can be added to find matches in a more automated way. The strongest conversion goal for a matchmaker business is the completion of a transaction after a successful match.

For a promotion business purchases can be a conversion goal, but it is more typical for customer acquisition and lead generation to be the most important activity. A contact form request or a newsletter signup are the most common conversion goals, but product information downloads or content views can also be valuable. Signing up for a deal or discount is a popular conversion goal.

Promotion businesses can seek out customer leads, but might also try to acquire leads for suppliers, partners, or sponsors via specialized appeals and contact forms. Advertisements for other businesses are not usually a good conversion goal because they are distracting and have an objective of customers clicking away somewhere else rather than becoming a lead for the business being promoted. Generating phone calls or live chats are particularly valuable customer leads for local businesses.

Milestone: Prototype and Analytics That Implement Digital Business Design

The first major milestone in digital entrepreneurship is creating a digital business design. The second major milestone is the creation of a prototype which implements the digital business design. When the prototype is built and linked to web analytics with defined conversion goals, then the digital entrepreneur is ready to test a new business idea on potential customers.

When the prototype is ready, do a quick check using the digital business design in each of the following areas:

- *Business goals and objective*—Looking at the prototype, is it obvious what type of business this is? Is the customer value proposition clearly expressed?

- *Competitors*—Compare the prototype to your closest competitor. Is it obvious how your prototype might do something differently, or better?

- *Acquisition*—Is your keyword search phrase featured in site content? Does the phrase bring enough visitors to contribute to your visitors/month goal? Is there social media content with an appropriate link to the site?

- *Behavior*—Does the domain name match the design? Does the most important use case work correctly, without errors?

- *Conversions*—Can a successful conversion be seen in the web analytics reports?

- *Conversion equation*—Is the projected conversion rate reasonable, given the performance of other similar sites?

Once the prototype is ready to go, it's time to test a business design, learn from it, and improve it if we can. We can do this by attracting more visitors, improving usability, and running experiments.

Additional Resources

https://premium.wpmudev.org/blog/google-tag-manager/—background on Google Tag Manager.
https://support.google.com/tagmanager/topic/7679108—list of triggers that can be tracked in Google Tag Manager.
www.newfoundmarketing.ca/track-youtube-views-with-google-tag-manager/—instructions for tracking video plays in Google Tag Manager.
https://unbounce.com/landing-page-articles/what-is-a-landing-page/—landing page definition and tips.
www.smartinsights.com/ecommerce/ecommerce-analytics/ecommerce-conversion-rates/—data on typical conversion rates for Ecommerce sites.
https://optinmonster.com/reasons-your-ecommerce-site-has-a-low-conversion-rate/—more discussion of how to improve conversion rates.

Exercises

9.1. Define the most important conversion goal for your prototype digital business site. Discuss why this goal is the most important.

9.2. For your chosen conversion goal, find evidence of a conversion rate experienced by a comparable business, or by sites generally.

9.3. Discuss whether the main conversion goal for your prototype site is better implemented as a destination goal or an event goal in Google Analytics.

9.4. Implement the main conversion goal of your prototype digital business as either a destination goal or an event goal.

9.5. Using real time reporting, show that conversion goal tracking is working on your prototype site.

9.6. Compare a completed prototype to its digital business design and make any necessary changes required to match the prototype to the design.

References

[1] F. Alhlou, S. Asif, and E. Fettman, *Google Analytics Breakthrough: From Zero to Business Impact*. Hoboken, NJ: John Wiley & Sons, 2016.

[2] T. Ash, M. Ginty, and R. Page, *Landing Page Optimization: The Definitive Guide to Testing and Tuning for Conversions*. Indianapolis, Indiana: John Wiley & Sons, 2012.

[3] D. Croxen-John and J. van Tonder, *E-Commerce Website Optimization: Why 95 Per Cent of Your Webiste Visitors Don't Buy and What You Can Do About It*. London: Kogan Page, 2017.

[4]   B. Schwerdt, *How to Build an Online Business*. Milton, Queensland: John Wiley & Sons, 2018.

[5]   B. Clifton, *Advanced Web Metrics with Google Analytics*. Indianapolis, Indiana: John Wiley & Sons, 2012.

[6]   A. Kaushik, *Web Analytics 2.0: The Art of Online Accountability and Science of Customer Centricity*. Indianapolis, Indiana: Wiley Publishing, 2011.

Usability and Customer Experience

Highlights

Chapter 10 introduces usability and customer experience improvement as a way to develop business prototypes.

- Usability and customer experience are important concepts for improving digital business ideas.

- In usability testing, customers are asked to perform specific tasks. By observing users, designers can identify barriers to successfully completing actions that lead to business success.

- This chapter shows how to design and conduct two basic types of usability tests.

- The end product of a usability test is a ranked list of the most important changes to make on a prototype site that will increase usability.

- Improving usability should lead to a better customer experience, more user satisfaction, and more conversions.

Improving Usability and Customer Experience

Usability is how easy a product or service is to use and learn how to use better in order to achieve goals that users care about. Perceived ease of use is an important issue for any product or service, but it is particularly crucial for new technology adoption. Trying a new technology is costly in terms of time and resources, potentially risky, and may disrupt existing ways of doing things. Making things easier to use is one of the most powerful tools entrepreneurs have to promote something new. Usability helps new products and services get over that initial barrier of convincing busy people to try something outside of their usual routine.

For online interactions in the digital world, usability is life or death. If a site or app isn't easy to use, people leave. If potential customers can't figure out how to do something they care about on their own, they bounce away, never to convert, and probably never to return. There are millions of other places to visit online only a click away.

On the positive side, usability is a tremendous opportunity for digital entrepreneurs. The digital world excels at providing easy access to just the right information or a connection with just the right people, to serve customers better. The biggest names in digital business, companies like Apple, Amazon, and Netflix, have all put usability at the core of their business success making phone gestures, one-click purchasing, and continuous binge watching incredibly easy—and incredibly lucrative.

Seemingly minor changes in usability can make a big difference in terms of business success or even life success. For example, a website that helped depressed people create a plan for coping with suicidal thoughts improved its usability in simple ways. The site updated how its instructions were written and changed a few confusing open-ended questions on a survey to multiple choice. The improved website raised completion rates for the plan and drastically reduced suicide-related emergency room admissions [1]. Usability can make money, but usability can also help the world in many other areas such as health, education, and government.

Usability is not a static thing, however, because customer goals change and products and services become more complex over time. Usability can slip even at an Apple (iTunes!) or an Amazon (mobile app!) as technologies change, more diverse user goals are served at the same time, and consistency has to be preserved with older, legacy technologies. Digital entrepreneurs can start with a blank screen, a laser-like focus on a targeted customer niche, and an ability to change quickly.

Usability of a product or service is traditionally thought of as part of an entire *customer experience*. Customer experience is the entire interaction and relationship that a customer has with a business across a customer journey, resulting in the completion of a meaningful goal. Meaningful goals might include becoming a new customer, making changes to an account, or resolving a problem. The customer experience can include interactions across many different touch points in the pre-purchase stage, the purchase stage, and the post-purchase stage [2].

In traditional companies, customer experience can degrade as customers are handed off between many different people and different channels [3]. For example, starting utility service at a new home might be unsatisfying because an appointment time set with an online representative does not match the time given to the utility worker at your door, even if both the call center person and the worker are nice and helpful individually [4]. Digital entrepreneurs have an opportunity to make end-to-end customer journeys better either by replacing them or by working with existing companies to improve critical parts of the process.

Usability Testing

In *usability testing* customers are asked to perform specific tasks while being observed. By observing users, designers can identify any barriers to successfully completing actions that lead to business success. Test subjects are often asked to speak aloud and answer questions, but watching what they do is just as important as listening to what they say.

Usability tests are one of the best things people can do to improve web sites or customer experiences generally [5]. While web analytics data answers questions about what visitors are doing on a site, usability tests can help answer the 'why' questions. Why are visitors getting lost or confused here? Why isn't this site meeting expectations? Why are visitors tempted to leave?

Usability experts argue that early, rapid, and repeated testing is more valuable than one-time tests on lots of people [5]. Consistent with the Minimum Viable Product philosophy, usability testing should be done early in the prototyping process before a site is 'finished', in order to maximize learning. While recruiting perfectly representative users as test subjects is always nice, the more important issue is to test with fresh pairs of eyes. Most usability problems can be found by anyone.

The end result of a usability test is a list of proposed fixes for the most important usability problems identified in the tests. The first priority is to find fixes that can be made quickly and easily. Sometimes a simple change of text or layout will improve usability. One of the big tradeoffs in usability, however, is balancing the need to solve usability problems by adding more things—more help, more directions, more options—with not making a site so complex and crowded that ease of use suffers. Better usability for certain tasks is great but it cannot overcome confusion about what a site is and what its customers are trying to achieve.

If a prototype site is still too basic for much usability testing, it can be helpful to perform a usability test on a competitor site. A test on a competitor is always incomplete in the sense that fixes cannot be made on someone else's site, but competitor testing can find valuable opportunities for making your own prototype easier to use. And it's never a bad idea to understand your competition better.

Quick Usability Tests

Quick usability tests perform a fixed task in a short period of time. Some are intended to overcome the bounce problem: the high likelihood that visitors will bounce, or leave immediately, in the first few seconds if it is not clear what a site does. Quick usability tests include:

Napkin test—named after the mythical startup activity of scribbling business plans on napkins in Silicon Valley diners. In a napkin test, a person is shown a crude drawing of a prototype site and asked: 'What do you think this is supposed to be?' The test subject then describes what they believe the purpose of the site is and points to parts of the napkin explaining why they came to that conclusion. If a prototype site is already built, a napkin test can be performed by looking at a screen with the home page or at important landing pages.

Five second test—similar to a napkin test. A person is shown a prototype site for five seconds. The site is hidden or taken away, and the person is asked to make a list of what they can remember about the site. This test can also reveal whether the main message of the site, and its purpose, is getting across.

Wireframe test—a wireframe is a single page mockup of a site or app where menu items and text headings are labeled, but areas of the screen where text and images will appear are filled with random text or an 'x'. The wireframe is shown to a person and asked: 'How would you find "something"?' where 'something' is a content or feature that is important for customer satisfaction and conversion. Wireframe tests are best for resolving navigation, categorization, and naming problems.

The result of a quick usability test should be a proposed change to a prototype. The proposed change should make the prototype easier to understand, use, or navigate. The change should be described with enough detail that someone else could make the change on their own without requiring additional information.

It is important to remember that a quick usability test is still a usability test, not an opinion survey. A usability test tries to provide an objective standard for making a prototype better. A prototype is better when a customer can complete a task more successfully. Opinions are also valuable input but they can be contradictory and send your improvement efforts in different directions. Be sure that you complete the more objective part of any usability test by observing user activity and finding the reasons for good or poor task performance before there are any conversations about what users like or don't like.

Full Usability Tests

A proper usability test involves watching people try to complete important tasks using your prototype site, with the intention of making it easier to use. Even sites from the biggest name tech companies have usability problems, and most of these problems are easily found by visitors who are not involved in the project. Watching potential customers try to use a product or service is valuable for any entrepreneur but is especially important for digital entrepreneurs because their customer interactions are almost entirely self-service.

In a usability test, a person is given a task to complete in the form of a scenario or a short, written description of the task they need to perform, together with the additional information and context needed to successfully complete the task. Test subjects are asked to speak aloud while they are completing the task to help reveal their thought process, especially when things break down. The usability test can be performed in person with an observer guiding the test subject and encouraging them to speak aloud. Or a test can be performed remotely, with a test subject being recorded while they try to complete the task and answer pre-defined questions.

The most important decision in usability testing is choosing the right task. The task should be important for business success. Normally, the main use case from the digital business design is a good starting point, or you can create a list of the five to ten most important things that people need to do with your prototype and select from that list.

A good task should be realistic and help a customer achieve an important goal. Examples of tasks include:

- Find a babysitter.

- Learn about the benefits of a new product.

- Purchase a sweater that is on sale.

- Contact a sales representative for an appointment.

A task might end with a conversion goal, but for many digital businesses actions on the way to the goal might be more important to test than the conversion itself. For example, making a purchase by putting something in a shopping cart is usually easy, but finding the right product or the reason why a product should be bought at this store might be more difficult. Clicking on an advertisement may be the conversion goal of a content-based business but clicking on ads is unlikely to have usability problems, at least compared to providing the right content that will satisfy customers, and is organized in the right way.

Once a task is chosen, then it is written up as a scenario for a test subject. A scenario gives the motivation for achieving a goal and additional information that allows the test subject to complete as realistic a task as possible. A good scenario will be specific enough that success or failure can be evaluated objectively. For example, 'find an orange sweater under $40' can be assessed more objectively than 'find your favorite sweater'. Example scenarios for the preceding tasks might be:

- 'You are young parents looking to find a new babysitter for your six year old next Saturday night from 6pm to 10pm. Find a babysitter that is available, and request them'.

- 'You are a local business interested in finding a new accounting service. Find the top three reasons why existing customers switch to this new accounting service'.

- 'You are looking for a sweater for your sister's birthday, but it needs to be on sale. Find a green sweater, medium size, on sale for $40 or less'.

- 'Contact a sales representative to discuss buying supplies for a new local restaurant'.

If the context isn't clear, it can be helpful to write a persona for your customer which includes their background, their interests, and their goals [6]. A good scenario describes what a real customer is trying to do, in their own language. A scenario should be written clearly enough that a test subject can read, understand, and follow it on their own. It should provide all the information a test subject needs.

A common mistake in scenarios is to provide specific instructions using unusual or technical terms that might appear on a screen. Telling a user to 'find the contact us menu, click on it, fill out the form, and click the "submit" button' is not a good scenario, because it provides a detailed set of instructions a typical customer would not have when they arrive at a prototype. This kind of scenario only tests whether people can find the right words on a screen, when the usability problem might be that the words themselves are confusing or wrong. A scenario should not give away how the user interface will be used. Don't use unusual terms that appear on a screen in a scenario.

For an in-person usability test, put the test subject in front of the prototype and have them read aloud (or read to them) the scenario. Ask the test subject to speak out loud as they are using the prototype. The observer should try to interfere as little as possible. If the test subject is stuck, encourage them to look around, try something else, and fully explain their confusion out loud. The observer should only help a test subject overcome a usability problem when they are certain that they fully understand the source of confusion and the test subject has tried all other options. Keep questions to a minimum, but if at any time it is not clear why a test subject is doing something, ask them to speak their thoughts out loud. More open-ended and opinion-based questions can be saved for the end.

Remote usability tests are fantastically convenient, because of their ability to instantly recruit as many test subjects as desired. For remote testing it is sometimes useful to break up a large scenario into smaller subtasks so that if a test subject becomes stuck they can still provide data on other aspects of the prototype. Some of the more important questions to ask remote test subjects include:

- Were you able to complete your task? If you were not able to complete your task, why not?

- What would make completing your task easier?

- How satisfied were you with your site experience overall?

In addition to saving a recording of the session, the observer should take notes, with a particular focus on any moments when the test subject became frustrated or threatens to leave the prototype.

Usability Test Results and Fixes

As soon as possible after completion of the usability test, an entrepreneur should meet with other team members or trusted partners and have a debriefing session. The main outcome of the meeting is to list the most serious usability problems revealed by the test. Which problems are most serious? It's usually obvious, but a helpful guideline is to focus on issues that make a conversion less likely or cause a bounce. Many usability problems are caused by visitors starting with the wrong set of assumptions about what can be done on a site, so another guideline is to prioritize usability problems earlier in the process that may set the wrong expectations for the entire interaction.

Once the usability problems are identified and prioritized, choose no more than three problems to fix. For each problem, list the simplest fix possible or the smallest change that will address the usability problem found in the testing. Resist the temptation to focus on other site improvement ideas and address the test results only. Prioritize fixes that change or remove something on a screen over fixes that add more things to a screen. Making something easier to find can be achieved by making that thing more visible or by removing other things that distract. Try to remove distractions first.

Sometimes a more fundamental redesign will be required or new prototype features will need to be added, but try the simplest fixes first. Simple fixes have the advantage that they can be implemented immediately. Make the changes the same day, which will speed up the experimentation and learning process.

Updating the Prototype and Design

Ideally, a fix made after a usability test will result in a *closed-loop* improvement in performance. In a closed-loop improvement, performance is measured before and after a change and a significant improvement can be seen in the difference between the two. The web analytics data might show improvements in bounce rate after a change, for example, or there might be an improvement in overall conversion rates. Part of the reason why usability testing should happen early and often is that seeing measurable improvements in the analytics data takes time, particularly for early prototypes with few visitors.

Usability testing is helpful for answering some of the 'why' questions raised by web analytics data. If visitors are spending a lot of time on a particular page, usability testing can reveal whether it is a sign of great interest or great confusion. Usability testing can explain why certain pages have high bounce rates and suggest fixes that will lead to performance improvements.

Sometimes, the simple fixes from usability testing will not produce sufficient improvement, either in the web analytics data or subsequent usability tests. The next step would be to provide new content or features that might address the issue. Bigger changes to a prototype might require changes to the digital business design itself by choosing a different use case, a new conversion goal, or even a 'pivot' to a completely new digital business idea. The difficult question of when to 'pivot' is discussed in Chapter 12.

Better usability is a great business opportunity for digital entrepreneurs. New customer needs expose usability problems in existing products and services. New devices, such as mobile phones and home voice assistants, often have terrible usability in their early phases. For a digital business to succeed, customers have to be comfortable interacting with the business in a way that's fundamentally different than previous in-person business interactions. Mastering the simple process of usability testing, fixing, and measuring business outcomes is a powerful entrepreneurial capability in the digital era.

Additional Resources

www.usability.gov/how-to-and-tools/methods/usability-testing.html—background on usability testing.

www.nngroup.com/articles/usability-101-introduction-to-usability/—detailed definition of usability.

www.peachpit.com/articles/article.aspx?p=1433954&seqNum=3—description of the 'napkin' test for usability.

www.nngroup.com/articles/task-scenarios-usability-testing/—tips for writing good usability testing scenarios.

www.usability.gov/how-to-and-tools/methods/scenarios.html—more examples of scenarios; we focus on the shorter goal- and task-based scenarios.

www.nngroup.com/articles/design-thinking/—background on the design thinking movement, and its ties to usability and prototyping.

https://uxdesign.cc/finding-my-way-through-the-amazon-c176509bfc23—example of how even the most successful digital businesses have usability issues; in this case, an Amazon mobile app.

www.fastcompany.com/3053406/how-apple-is-giving-design-a-bad-name—argument that even Apple, known for its design prowess, can wrongly prioritize good looks over usability.

www.nngroup.com/articles/intelligent-assistant-usability/—usability problems with new voice interfaces to intelligent assistants such as Alexa and Siri.

www.usertesting.com/—popular service for remote usability testing.

Exercises

10.1. Perform one of the quick usability tests on either your prototype site or on a drawing of its home page. Identify the most important change you would make to your prototype to reduce the bounce rate.

10.2. Write a scenario for a usability test of your digital business prototype site.

10.3. Describe the lessons learned from a usability test of your prototype site with at least three test subjects.

10.4. Implement the most important usability improvement on your prototype site as identified by a usability test. Discuss the performance improvement you expect to see in future analytics data or usability tests.

10.5. Perform a usability test on a competitor site. Discuss the opportunities for your digital business to improve on a competitor's usability.

References

[1]   E. D. Boudreaux, G. K. Brown, B. Stanley, R. S. Sadasivam, C. A. Camargo Jr, and I. W. Miller, "Computer Administered Safety Planning for Individuals at Risk for Suicide: Development and Usability Testing," *Journal of Medical Internet Research*, vol. 19, no. 5, 2017.

[2]   K. N. Lemon and P. C. Verhoef, "Understanding Customer Experience Throughout the Customer Journey," *Journal of Marketing*, vol. 80, no. 6, pp. 69–96, 2016.

[3]   A. Rawson, E. Duncan, and C. Jones, "The Truth About Customer Experience," *Harvard Business Review*, vol. 91, no. 9, pp. 90–98, 2013.

[4]   McKinsey & Company. *The Ceo Guide to Customer Experience*. (2016), available: www.mckinsey.com/business-functions/operations/our-insights/the-ceo-guide-to-customer-experience. [Accessed: August 1, 2018].

[5]   S. Krug, *Rocket Surgery Made Easy*. Berkeley, CA: New Riders, 2010.

[6]   D. Croxen-John and J. van Tonder, *E-Commerce Website Optimization: Why 95 Per Cent of Your Webiste Visitors Don't Buy and What You Can Do About It*. London: Kogan Page, 2017.

Chapter 11 Customer Acquisition in a Digital World

Highlights

Chapter 11 discusses how to attract online customers to a digital business prototype.

- Attracting new customers online is becoming a vital skill for all businesses, digital or not.

- Attracting customers in the digital world means competing with hundreds of millions of other web sites and apps.

- The most important customer acquisition channels include search, social media, paid advertisements, and email marketing.

- Search engines are a major source of potential customers online, with high conversion potential. Placement in the most relevant search rankings is critical, making search engine optimization an important activity.

- Social media is a fast-growing source of customers online. A social media customer acquisition strategy includes a content strategy, an engagement strategy, and an influencer strategy.

- A digital business should have clear customer acquisition goals, with a specific numeric target for each channel.

The New World of Customer Acquisition

There are few things more basic to business success than getting customers. The job of finding new customers is transforming in the digital era. The full set of digital marketing options, from search engines to social media influencers, from real-time advertising bids to affiliate networks, has made new customer acquisition more complex but has also created many opportunities for digital entrepreneurs.

Traditional marketing techniques for understanding customers, communicating with them, and delivering products are being challenged by digital technologies. If there is one theme that differentiates digital marketing from previous times, it is the richness of interactions that customers can now have not only with a business, but also with each other. Ryan argues that 'digital marketing is about people communicating with other people' [1].

Whether it's online reviews, social media influencers, official product information, or homemade how-to videos, potential customers turn to digital information the majority of the time for product research and purchase decisions. Before making an in-store purchase, 82% of smartphone users consult their phones [2]; 82% of Americans consult online reviews before purchasing something for the first time [3]; 86% of Americans want to compare prices or look for discounts online; and 84% want to be able to ask questions before a purchase. Information from business websites and online customer reviews are some of the most trusted sources of product information, ranked only behind personal recommendations [4]. In Business-to-Business sales (B2B), the effects are even stronger—nearly 100% of business customers do online research before considering a purchase [5].

Digital marketing is a big topic. Our interest as digital entrepreneurs testing a new digital business prototype will be to use one aspect of it: attracting a sufficient number of high quality visitors. The sufficient number is determined by the conversion equation in the current digital business design. High quality visitors are the ones who are more likely to convert. Some digital channels will be more effective in generating visitor traffic, and some efforts will be more effective than others in creating high quality traffic that will convert. The digital entrepreneur's job is to find those channels and those efforts that work best for 'steadily and reliably get[ting] targeted traffic to your website' [1].

Search

For many digital businesses, search engines such as Google are the single largest source of visitors. For big online retailers, unpaid or *organic* search results provide over a third of all visits on average, while paid advertising that appears next to search results provides another quarter of all visits [6]. Not surprisingly, visitors from search are often higher quality and provide more revenue because they are actively looking for business information. By knowing the visitor's *query*, or the phrase used in the search, it is often possible to guess the intent behind the search. Search intent makes it easier to serve a customer's needs and discover new, previously unserved needs.

The key thing about search from a customer acquisition standpoint is that it is largely a *winner-take-all* game. Potential customers are much more likely to click through and visit a digital business if it is a top search result. The top search result averages a 30% click through rate, declining to 15% on average for the second position, 10% for third, and down to 5% by position number five [7]. At the bottom of the first page of search results, by position number nine or ten, the average click through rate is 2% or less. The second page of search results are seen by few and clicked on by even fewer.

Unless your prototype is a top search result, the search channel will not generate new customer traffic. For digital entrepreneurs just starting, the challenge is to find the search queries where it is possible to be a top search result but that also generates enough traffic to give your prototype a proper test. In general, popular searches tend to have more competition, though the pool of people on the Internet worldwide is vast enough that new opportunities constantly arise for targeting search queries that have not yet spotted or served by the competition.

Becoming a Top Search Result

How can your business prototype become a top search result? The first step is for a search engine to know that your site exists. Google and other search engines have software that regularly downloads, or *crawls*, all of the web pages it knows about and follows all the links it finds on every page. If the search engine finds new pages it didn't know about before, it adds them to the database. The URL of a new site can also be submitted to a search engine. At Google this can be done through the Google Search Console.

Once a search engine knows about your web site it *indexes* every page to associate it with a set of keywords and phrases that it finds on the page. When a search query is entered, the search engine can find every page on the entire web indexed with those same terms. Any common phrase is likely to return many millions of results. For example, entering the query 'baby squirrels' in Google returns over 20 million pages as of this writing.

But how does a search engine decide which of the 20 million indexed pages will appear at the top of the search results? Why is a page at squirrelsandmore.com on baby squirrel care the top result for 'baby squirrels' and not the page at citywildlife.org, currently in position number ten?

Search result order is determined by the all-important *ranking* algorithm. Each search engine has its own ranking algorithm. Google says that over 200 factors are considered in their rankings. The algorithms are constantly changing, much of it in response to people trying to game the system and move their pages to the top of the rankings. And the most interesting part is, the search engines won't say exactly how the algorithms work, thus giving rise to the dark arts of *search engine optimization*, or SEO, where experts try to reverse engineer the constantly changing, secret algorithms and use any means possible to move pages up the search rankings at the expense of the competition.

The factors that affect search rankings can be divided roughly into *internal* and *external* SEO factors. Internal factors have to do with the design of your web page and are under your control. For example, the exact search query, or something very close to it, should be included in prominent places on a page such as in the page title, page headings, navigation links, or even within the URL. Other internal factors are more about evaluating the quality of the page overall, such as sites that use the more secure https: protocol instead of just http:, content that is refreshed more regularly, or sites that are optimized for mobile screens versus sites that are not.

External SEO factors are outside of your page design and to a greater extent are outside of your control. The main external factor are the links from other pages to your page. Links from other high quality, relevant pages will increase your page's search ranking. Other external factors, both positive and negative, might include click through rates to your site from previous web searches, the presence of content copied from other sites, or links from known spammers and SEO manipulators.

Keyword Strategy

The search engine companies will say that the best SEO strategy is to focus on creating the best original content possible, update it regularly, and the rest will take care of itself. Other sites will recognize the quality of your content and link to it over time. There is some truth in this. Great content is powerful for customer acquisition. Some formats, such as a WordPress blog, naturally encourage good search practices by encouraging the creation of original content, regular updates, and automatically generated titles and URLs that incorporate meaningful phrases that customers are likely to search for.

The highly competitive, winner-take-all nature of search results, however, means that many businesses take a more deliberate approach to targeting searches that will bring in potential customers and not have too much competition. The targeting of search phrases is known as a keyword strategy, named after the *keywords*, or the most important words in a search query.

The first task in a keyword strategy is choosing the keyword, or keywords, to target. Normally this begins with an entrepreneur's own idea about how a potential customer would phrase a search query, but you could also brainstorm a list of potential search queries with a small group or ask potential customers in person how they might search for your product or service. Services such as wordtracker.com and moz.com offer free trials of keyword search tools that will generate a list of related search queries to consider as your main target.

Google Ads provides a keyword planning tool that gives vital information about each potential search phrase: how many searches per month, the level of competition, and the cost per click for an advertisement that appears next to search results. After signing up for Google Ads, choose 'Tools' at the top of screen, then 'Keyword Planner'. For example, the search query 'baby squirrel' has at the time of writing 10–100k monthly searches, or somewhere between ten and a hundred thousand. And it has 'low' competition. As long as the search query implies a customer intent that might realistically lead to a conversion, a search query with high traffic and low competition is a great place to start. A search query with zero searches per month cannot drive any traffic to your prototype site, so it should not be the target of your keyword strategy.

A keyword planner tool also provides other ideas for search queries to target. Other related search queries with high traffic and lower competition include 'what to feed a baby squirrel' and 'what do baby squirrels eat', which might be reasonable alternatives. The cost per click advertising price is useful information for planning purposes. If paid advertising is a possibility in the future to quickly increase visitor numbers, then a phrase with a lower cost per click is a good choice. The two preceding similar search queries have very different advertising costs. The only exception would be if the revenue model for a digital business is advertisement publishing. In that case, an entrepreneur would seek out the phrase with a higher cost, hoping to earn more revenue for each ad click by a visitor.

Once a keyword or keywords are chosen, steps can be taken to improve internal, or on-site, SEO, and external SEO, which happens off-site. At its most basic, implementing good SEO helps avoid obvious mistakes and gives a prototype its best chance at winning the search ranking game. More precisely, SEO reveals the level of performance necessary to beat the competition. To rank higher than another site on a search query, either the internal SEO or external SEO has to be better, or both.

Implementing Internal SEO

The most important task for internal SEO is to make sure that the exact keywords and phrase being targeted are on the site and in the right places. Ranking algorithms prioritize keywords and phrases in special locations on a page. Make sure your keywords are featured in places such as:

- Page title.

- URL.

- Prominent places on page, such as headers.

- In HTML <meta> tags, which define information about a page such as keywords and a short description.

- In the 'alt' attribute of HTML <img> tags for images.

It can also be helpful for the links within a site, such as the menus and navigation, to consistently point to a single page on site that is associated with a keyword or keyword phrase. This can be implemented by having the link text include the keywords. For WordPress-based sites, one of the most popular types of plugin is for better SEO. These plugins highlight common problems, mostly with internal SEO, and suggest fixes.

As ranking algorithms change, new internal SEO factors will rise or fall in importance. For example, search engines have been more concerned recently with the problem of web sites copying content from other sites. The search rankings now put some weight on whether Google believes your site has original content or content copied from others. Other more technical aspects, such as having a mobile-friendly site, or using the 'https:' rather than the 'http:' protocol, are new internal SEO factors that have to be responded to and provide opportunities for new entrants.

Implementing External SEO

External SEO is largely an issue of having links from other sites. The best links are from other sites that are themselves highly ranked. To win an external SEO competition, your prototype site needs to have comparable or better links than another competitor site. A tool such as the moz.com Open Site Explorer will give information for any site about how many *inbound links* it has, or links from other sites, along with a reputation score. This tool estimates the reputation assigned by the search rankings to a page or domain with an inbound link to a site. Your competitive task is to meet or beat the inbound link quality of your competition.

Other sites are not under your control, of course, so one approach is to sit back, create great content, and wait for other good sites to recognize your quality and link to you. A more proactive first step is to link to your prototype site from other sites or profiles that you control. Create business pages on social media platforms and profiles on business directories and be sure there is a link to your site, preferably mentioning the keywords from your strategy in the text of the link.

Next, think about finding other reputable sites that will include a link to yours. There may be specialized news sites in your area of interest, or established bloggers who need content. Approaching these targets, especially with already-created content their readers will find useful, can be helpful. Discussion boards or online communities can be other places to naturally include links to your prototype, though some have restrictions on self-promotion. Mutually beneficial exchanges of links are common, but any links that are paid for outright will be penalized in the search results if a search engine company finds out about it. Getting links from other reputable sites takes creativity, hustle, and sometimes luck, but it is difficult to win the search ranking game without them.

Social Media

Social media isn't the largest channel for bringing customers to retail sites, but it is the fastest growing. For certain niches and demographics, social media is a natural fit for acquiring customers. Social media is a big generator of visitor traffic overall, perhaps up to a third of all web traffic [1]. Social media is especially appropriate for more unique, personalized consumer products that tie to people's identity or personal values [8].

Social media includes the big-name platforms such as Facebook and Instagram, but also includes specialized platforms such as LinkedIn and Pinterest, content sites with community discussion such as YouTube and Reddit, and review and rating sites. With marketing shifting to more conversational modes, rather than broadcasts, there are many potential marketing uses of social media. Social media can help build brand awareness, find influencers and brand advocates, support customers, learn about customer needs, and shape public relations in ways that newer companies can take advantage of.

Because social media is so conversational, it can be time consuming, raising the question of whether the return on investment on social media activity is worthwhile for businesses. While social engagement has many business uses, our interest in social media will focus on customer acquisition. Social media is effective for our business prototypes to the extent to which it 'steadily and reliably get[s] targeted traffic to your website' [1].

With this goal in mind, successful social media use has parallels to search in terms of how customers find us (discovery), how messages spread (virality), appropriate content (content mix), and appropriate timing (timeline), as shown in Table 11.1:

Table 11.1 Customer Acquisition Issues in Search and Social Media

Issue	Search	Social Media
Discovery	Search queries; keyword phrases; changing search ranking algorithms	Hashtags; changing news feed ranking algorithms
Virality	Inbound links from high reputation sites	Network connections; influencers
Content Mix	Short vs. long form; images and video	Sales vs. education vs. entertainment
Timeline	Regularly updated original content	Posting frequency; time of day

Like search, customer acquisition with social media benefits from using key phrases that are trending. One of the challenges of search result visibility is being connected to other sites with high reputations. In social media, promoting content through developed networks and key influencers is a major issue. Finding the right types of content is a challenge, as explored in Chapter 5, but the right balance of sales information versus educational and entertainment content is especially important in social media because its more conversational style changes customer expectations. Search rankings reward content that is regularly updated, but social media timing rewards more precision, with concerns about day of the week, time of day, and how often posts are updates for maximum attention.

Social Media Strategy

A social media strategy for attracting visitors to a prototype site includes three related aspects: a content strategy, an engagement strategy, and an influencer strategy.

The content strategy defines the mix of commercial, educational, and entertainment content, as well as post frequency and timing. Social media content is more effective when it is not just a stream of commercial messages. Content that connects emotionally, sparks conversations, raises questions, or makes people feel good about themselves tends to have more reach on social media [8]. Images are important, and strange or noteworthy images seem to be tolerated more on social media than other channels.

The engagement strategy is the plan for getting customers to follow a social media account and then engage with its content by sharing, liking, and commenting. Engagement has business benefits for its own sake, but engagement is also critical for content visibility on social media platforms because of the algorithms deciding which content appear at the top of news feeds. Messages with high quality arguments that attract more likes and comments and that are considered admirable and appealing are more likely to be liked and shared [9].

Unless followers regularly interact with content, it is much less likely to be seen in customer news feeds, even if these customers already follow the business [8]. Of course, if potential customers are not following a social media account, they are unlikely to see its content at all. Inducements such as discounts or premium content can be offered in exchange for following.

The influencer strategy is the plan for quickly spreading content through a social media network. A small set of people, known as influencers, have much more visibility on social media than others due to their massive followings. Influencers are trusted almost as much as personal recommendations in terms of product endorsements and fit better with how many social media users like to learn about new products and services. The biggest influencers will demand serious compensation for their services, but there can be niche influencers who are open to a more modest request. To convince a niche influencer, try to bring them something unique and engaging for their audience—just like you, they need a steady stream of content to keep their followers interested. Check out an influencer's history, and if there's a good match make a personal approach.

Email Marketing

There are many other sources of online customers besides search and social media. We briefly discuss four other channels: email, paid advertising, word of mouth, and e-commerce marketplaces.

In *email marketing*, email addresses are collected from potential customers, who are then sent regular newsletters. Links in the newsletters bring visitors back to a prototype site. Email marketing is simple, inexpensive, and has high conversion rates, which is why digital businesses go to great lengths to collect email addresses, including the ever-popular pop-up request during a site visit.

Email is one of the most highly efficient marketing channels [10], often outperforming other more expensive marketing sources [1]. People willing to give an email address already have some connection with your business and are more likely to convert. The top tip from almost all guides to 'getting rich quick on the Internet!' is to build the email list.

Typically, an outside service is used for email marketing. Specialized services know how to get around the spam filters which stop around 90% of all emails. Outside services can track how often mailboxes are opened in inboxes, manage subscriptions, and send higher volumes of mail more quickly than the email servers available on a shared hosting service. Newsletter plugins are available for WordPress sites that are appropriate for testing small email lists.

In terms of newsletter content, an inverted pyramid format like a classic news article is recommended. The subject line is the compelling hook, just like an article headline. Give the main message first, then go into the details, because many email readers give a summary or preview based on the beginning of the message. Don't neglect proofreading—hold newsletter content to the same quality level as site content. Using links with custom URLs or unique landing pages allows the effectiveness of each newsletter to be tracked in web analytics.

Newsletter content can either be treated more like a direct mail sales exercise or as another type of social media with a mix of commercial, educational, and entertainment content. The social media approach provides general information, tips and how-tos, and customer stories, along with sales pitches and calls to action. Allowing customers to choose from a set of specialized alerts or topics can be a helpful involvement tactic.

A pure direct mail approach will try to create a click by using 'bait' to capture attention, an argument why a product or service can solve a problem, and an immediate call to action, the standard persuasion tools of direct mail. In a direct mail approach, the text would also try to motivate customer action by generating emotional responses such as fear, followed by guilt, greed (discounts and low price), and exclusivity [11].

Paid Advertising

Most customer acquisition channels—search, social media, and email—take time to build. Paid advertising is an effective tool for generating customer visits quickly. Common outlets for paid advertising include search ads, website ads, and social media ads. Paid search ads are one of the largest sources of retail shopping traffic online. The same tools used to find search keywords at Google Ads can be used to find search queries to advertise on, and an estimate of how much each ad click will cost.

Advertising campaigns can be set with either manual cost-per-click bids, or by specifying a ranking and letting the cost adjust automatically. Be sure to set a maximum spend on a campaign, because Internet ads can generate a lot of visitors very quickly, leading to a very expensive test. For the links back to the prototype site, use a customized URL for the campaign, or a unique landing page, to track the effectiveness of each advertisement.

Once a site has over a thousand visitors a month, *remarketing* can be used to customize advertisements based on previous visits, just like when you visit a shopping site one day and see nothing but ads for that site the rest of the week. Customers sometimes find remarketing advertisements intrusive if they feel they do not have control over how their personal information is shared [12].

Google has one of the largest advertising networks, but there are many other networks for publishing advertisements on web sites. Video ads are only about 10% the revenue of television advertising, at around $5 billion a year, but are growing quickly [1]. Categories of sites or individual sites can be blocked, if advertisements are being paired with inappropriate content. As tempting as it might be, do not click on your own advertisements, even in testing. This is called *click fraud*. If an advertising network suspects any fraudulent ad clicking activity, your account will be shut down immediately.

A third paid advertising option is social media. Social media ads have the advantage of precise targeting based on detailed demographics and interests. Advertisements can have engagement actions as a goal, such as likes, comments, and shares. Our emphasis is creating clicks back to a prototype site, again using a custom URL or landing page for tracking purposes.

Social media ads offer the choice of traditional display advertisements on the side, or promoted or 'boosted' content inside the news feed itself. Some experts claim that advertising content within a news feed is more effective [8], but this can be tested with experimentation.

Social media ads sometimes have to work a little harder to capture attention and to induce action away from the platform. The average social media user is exposed to over three thousand commercial messages per day. Any call to action will have to offer immediate and significant value, either in terms of discounts, information, or entertainment.

A different approach to paid advertisement is to use *affiliate marketing* and pay for results, not just clicks and visits. Affiliate marketing pays a referral fee for each successful conversion. Normally, an outside affiliate marketing service or network would be used to create an affiliate program and manage the process of setting cookies and paying commissions for the referrals. If customer leads are scarce, conversions are difficult, and an entrepreneur is willing to spend up to 50% of their profit margin for customer acquisition purposes, affiliate programs are an option to explore.

Word of Mouth Marketing

Word of mouth marketing through online reviews, in-person events, and old-fashioned publicity can be a powerful source of customers, even for a digital business. Every digital business should be soliciting reviews and testimonials from day one.

Entrepreneurs usually begin word of mouth marketing with their own networks and expand upon them using classic guerrilla marketing techniques such as free events, seminars, product demonstrations, and free consultations. Entrepreneurs can offer themselves as experts, writing articles themselves, and hiring others to write articles and research studies that will be picked up by the media. Classic public relations techniques include contacting journalists when a hot news story is related to your digital business, complete with a hook or story (including character development, conflict or adversity, and plot) that will capture widespread interest.

The impacts of word of mouth depend on how their language is perceived. Consumers find explanatory language more helpful and influential than simply opinions. Softer phrasing of negative opinions makes them more persuasive. Recent reviews are perceived as more valuable. And despite the common belief that social media is leading everyone to share their opinions about everything, consumers are actually less likely to share word of mouth recommendations over social media than in person because of the social risk involved [12].

Word of mouth takes more time and energy than money, which is a positive feature in the earliest phases of a business test but can be challenging to scale up much beyond the personal network. Try to use word of mouth not only as a customer acquisition channel itself but also to build reputation and a following in other channels that will generate new visitors more consistently.

E-Commerce Platforms

For digital businesses that depend on sales, placement on e-commerce platforms can drive visitor traffic. A platform like Amazon Marketplace will charge a 6–15% referral fee for each sale, plus a monthly subscription fee. Warehousing and fulfillment services are available for additional charges.

On e-commerce platforms, a massive audience comes with cutthroat competition. But with a unique enough product or service positioning, e-commerce platforms can provide a big customer acquisition boost. A Shopify, Etsy, or eBay store can attract additional customers, as well as provide useful storefront, payment, and fulfillment features.

Setting Customer Acquisition Goals

There are many different routes to customer acquisition in the digital world. The complexity of these new digital channels opens up possibilities for entrepreneurs. This chapter has barely scratched the surface of what is possible today in digital marketing. Many companies now try to improve customer acquisition across multiple channels, or *multichannel*. Acquisition and conversion activities are often more effective when messages and calls to action are seen across multiple channels. With additional tracking code and the use of custom URLs multichannel conversions can be tracked in web analytics.

From the perspective of testing a new digital business design, the important deliverable is a numeric target for each of the most important channels. How many visitors per month will each channel deliver to the prototype site? These targets, added together, are the first part of the conversion equation which, combined with conversion rate, will determine the success of the prototype.

Additional Resources

www.google.com/webmasters/tools/home—Google Search Console, for submitting site URLs for crawling.

https://adwords.google.com—Google advertising platform with keyword planner tool.

www.wordtracker.com—keyword idea search tool.

https://moz.com/learn/seo/what-are-keywords—background on search keywords.

https://moz.com/free-seo-tools—tools for keyword ideas and external SEO research.

www.w3schools.com/tags/tag_meta.asp—additional HTML tags for internal SEO.

www.w3schools.com/tags/att_img_alt.asp—HTML tag attribute for adding keywords to images.

https://moz.com/learn/seo/domain-authority—background on how sites build reputation in search results.

https://mailchimp.com/pricing/free/—example of an email marketing service with a free service level.

Exercises

11.1. Identify three potential keyword phrases as targets of a keyword strategy for your digital business. For each phrase, identify the page on the competitor site that will be replaced in the rankings a page from your prototype. Evaluate the SEO reputation of this competitor site.

11.2. Identify the three most important steps for implementing internal SEO on your prototype site. Implement these steps.

11.3. Find two other sites that are likely candidates for adding inbound links to your prototype site. Check that these sites have sufficient reputation to implement your SEO strategy. Describe the steps you would take to earn those inbound links.

11.4. Create a business social media profile for your digital business. Establish links in both directions between your social media profile and your prototype site.

11.5. Describe the social media content strategy for your digital business and the target number of visitors per month. Implement one week's worth of content on the social media account.

11.6. Identify the actions you will take in the first week to implement the social media engagement and influencer strategy for your digital business.

11.7. Choose at least one customer acquisition channel from this lesson and discuss why this customer acquisition channel might be more appropriate for your digital business prototype than either search or social media.

11.8. What is the overall customer acquisition goal for your digital business prototype, in terms of unique monthly visitors? How many visitors will each of the top two acquisition channels contribute toward this goal?

References

[1]   D. Ryan, *Understanding Digital Marketing: Marketing Strategies for Engaging the Digital Generation*. London: Kogan Page Publishers, 2016.

[2]   J. Ellett. *New Research Shows Growing Impact of Online Research on in-Store Purchases*. (2018), available: www.forbes.com/sites/johnellett/2018/02/08/new-research-shows-growing-impact-of-online-research-on-in-store-purchases/. [Accessed: August 10, 2018].

[3]   A. Smith and M. Anderson. *Online Shopping and E-Commerce*. (2016), available: www.pewinternet.org/2016/12/19/online-shopping-and-e-commerce/. [Accessed: August 10, 2018].

[4]   Nielsen. *Global Trust in Advertising*. (2015), available: www.nielsen.com/us/en/insights/reports/2015/global-

trust-in-advertising-2015.html. [Accessed: August 10, 2018].

[5]   Brafton Inc. *94 Percent of B2b Buyers Research Online for Purchase Decisions*. (2014), available: www.brafton. com/news/94-percent-b2b-buyers-research-online-purchase-decisions/. [Accessed: August 10, 2018].

[6]   Adobe Inc. *Adi Retail Industry Report—Q2 2017*. (2017), available: www.slideshare.net/adobe/adi-retail-industry-report-q2-2017. [Accessed: August 10, 2018].

[7]   D. Chaffey. *Comparison of Google Clickthrough Rates by Position*. (2018), available: www.smartinsights. com/search-engine-optimisation-seo/seo-analytics/comparison-of-google-clickthrough-rates-by-position/. [Accessed: August 10, 2018].

[8]   P. Marshall, K. Krance, and T. Meloche, *Ultimate Guide to Facebook Advertising: How to Access 1 Billion Potential Customers in 10 Minutes*, 2nd ed. Irvine, CA: Entrepreneur Press, 2015.

[9]   Y.-T. Chang, H. Yu, and H.-P. Lu, "Persuasive Messages, Popularity Cohesion, and Message Diffusion in Social Media Marketing," *Journal of Business Research*, vol. 68, no. 4, pp. 777–782, 2015.

[10] W. Reinartz, J. S. Thomas, and V. Kumar, "Balancing Acquisition and Retention Resources to Maximize Customer Profitability," *Journal of Marketing*, vol. 69, no. 1, pp. 63–79, 2005.

[11] R. Stim and L. Guerin, *Running a Side Business: How to Create a Second Income*. Berkeley, CA: Nolo, 2009.

[12] A. T. Stephen, "The Role of Digital and Social Media Marketing in Consumer Behavior," *Current Opinion in Psychology*, vol. 10, pp. 17–21, 2016.

Digital Business Experiments

Highlights

Chapter 12 discusses how to learn from customer data and experiments.

- Digital entrepreneurs have the advantage of being able to learn from experience quickly and cheaply as they search for a viable new business idea. With a prototype site, web analytics, and a digital business design digital entrepreneurs have the tools they need to test new business ideas.

- Web analytics has extensive acquisition, behavior, and conversion reports that can be used to improve each phase of the 'ABC' process.

- Content experiments, particularly A/B testing, are an important experimental tool. In an A/B test, visitors are sent randomly to different versions of a prototype to see which version leads to a higher conversion rate.

- A third major milestone in digital entrepreneurship is an updated digital business design and prototype based on the data from early experiments. The goal is to either make the original digital business idea more effective, change it, or abandon it gracefully with lessons learned.

Analyzing Customer Data

Is a business design a good one? Is the prototype attracting and satisfying visitors? Does it convert visitors into potential customers who either pay a business, or provide other kinds of value? Can the business design, and therefore the business idea itself, be improved? For answers to these questions, we turn to the world of digital business experiments. Digital entrepreneurs are fortunate to have at their disposal an unprecedented ability to try new things quickly and cheaply on a vast universe of potential customers.

A completed digital business prototype connected to web analytics is ready to test a new business idea, as implemented in a digital business design. Web analytics provides the all-important data about how the Minimum Viable Product (MVP) or service is performing with potential customers. The goal for digital entrepreneurs is to become skilled at the process of continuous experimentation and improvement: measuring a baseline of performance, trying new things, and seeing improvement in the data (or not). The reporting provided by web analytics is one of the main sources of performance data.

Reporting in Google Analytics is organized around the 'ABC' process: acquisition and audience reports, behavior reports, and conversion reports. Each type of report provides a different measurement of performance. The reports provide an ability not just to drill down on the details of each step of the process, but also to see how each step relates to the greater goal of conversion.

Audience Report Analysis

Audience reports in web analytics give entrepreneurs basic information about the number of visitors to a site and, subject to the measurement limitations discussed in Chapter 8, how often visitors return. Audience size is the first test of whether a business prototype is meeting the overall goal for customer acquisition, as written in its conversion equation. The number and frequency of returning visitors tells us about the level of sustained interest in the digital business so far. Stickiness, or the ratio of average daily users to total monthly users, is another commonly used indicator of how devoted regular users are to a digital business.

Audience reports can be used to scan for unexpected surprises, either positive or negative. Unexpected interest from a particular country might be a signal to create additional content or features with that nation's visitors in mind. Comparing visitor numbers across different devices can reveal where a business prototype might be falling short in terms of a mobile or tablet experience. The charts which compare audience numbers versus site-wide averages are particularly useful for finding areas of positive or negative surprise.

Linking Google Analytics with additional services can provide additional audience reporting. Signing up for benchmarking allows you to compare a prototype's performance data with other sites that Google considers similar to yours. By linking with Google advertising services, Google Analytics can use the data contained in its user profiles to break down visitors by demographic information (such as age and gender) and interests. Signing up for multichannel or cross channel reporting will enable reporting on user activities across multiple devices and advertising channels, as long as the visitors are logged in to Google.

The standard web analytics reports combine data on many different types of visitors. It can be more insightful to divide up the total audience into more specific *segments* for performance measurement purposes. For example, an entrepreneur may be much more concerned about the exit pages of visitors that do not convert than for visitors who do convert; combining data about the two might hide the exit pages that are specifically chasing non-converting visitors away.

Segmentation makes the analytics data more meaningful by focusing on specific kinds of users, each of which may have different sources, needs, and end goals [1] rather than aggregating all different kinds of visitors into a single measure. Common forms of segmentation include:

- Separating customers from non-customers, or converters from non-converters.

- Separating non-serious visitors that bounce away immediately from other visitors (also known as *non-bounced sessions*).

- Focusing on a particular user technology such as mobile users.

- Focusing on a particular geographic area.

- Focusing on visitors from a particular referral source.

- Focusing on customers who visited a specific page, for example a specific promotion or discount.

- Separating two different types of visitors in a matchmaking business such as potential service providers versus potential customers.

A segment can also be used to trigger *remarketing*, or the targeting of display ads about your business to recent visitors. For example, a segment of visitors that saw at least three pages on your site, but did not convert, could be the target of an immediate remarketing campaign on the Google Ads platform.

Acquisition Report Analysis

Acquisition reports tell the entrepreneur how many visitors are coming from each channel. Channels in Google Analytics include:

- *Direct*—typing a domain name or URL into a browser.

- *Organic search*—clicking on a search result from a known search engine.

- *Social*—clicking on a link from a known social platform.

- *Referral*—clicking on a link from another website that is not a search or social site.

- *Email*—clicking on a link in an email newsletter.

- *Paid search*—clicking on an advertisement displayed next to search results.

- *Display*—clicking on an advertisement from another site.

How successful are customer acquisition efforts from the most important channels? How is each channel contributing to the overall customer acquisition goal? Are there any surprises, positive or negative? These are the first questions to be answered by acquisition reports. Visitor reporting by medium uses a less detailed set of categories than channels, while source reporting is more specific, revealing the specific domain names that visitors are coming from. The 'Source/Medium' and 'Referrals' reports under 'All Traffic' in Google Analytics can reveal sites that are successfully generating visits, especially previously unknown sites.

The acquisition 'Overview' report may be the single most useful report in all of Google Analytics. It gives an overview of the entire 'ABC' process, showing which channels bring new or returning visitors, which channels bring visitors that don't bounce and do engage with the prototype, and most importantly which channels bring visitors that convert. The bounce rates and conversion rates can be quite different across channels. Attracting the most promising, high performing customers is a major part of digital business success.

As with the audience reports, linking to other Google services can provide additional insights. By linking to a Google Ads account, acquisition reports can identify the specific advertisements that bring in visitors and compare their performance in terms of bounce rates and conversion rates. By grouping advertisements into campaigns, web analytics can track the performance of different advertising approaches. Google Ads can automatically add parameters at the end of a URL to your prototype site to identify specific campaigns, or custom URLs can be created using a campaign URL builder.

One of the most powerful tools for analyzing customer acquisition is to see the exact search phrases that bring visitors to a site. By default, search phrase information does not appear in Google Analytics reports. However, by signing up for Google Search Console and entering your Google Analytics account information, as discussed in Chapter 11, the detailed search queries used by visitors will appear in the reporting. Search acquisition reports are useful for evaluating whether a search strategy is working, but equally importantly the search query data can identify new keywords and phrases that might be a target for future SEO activities.

Behavior Report Analysis

The behavior reports provide data about the user experience once visitors arrive. The 'Overview' report in Google Analytics provides the overall bounce rate and information about the most popular content. Bounce rates above an industry average, or above an absolute target such as 45–50% [2], are potentially cause for concern and additional investigation. The 'Behavior Flow' report can be used to see whether visitors are successfully navigating the most important use case in the digital business design, or if they are being taken away to other parts of the prototype. Behavior flow surprises can be positive or negative, depending on whether the newly discovered pathways are leading to conversions or not.

Under 'Site Content', detailed reports can reveal bounce rates and exit rates for all pages. Pages that generate high bounce rates or exit rates are candidates for repair or replacement [3]. Unexpectedly popular pages can be a signal to build more content or features along those lines. When prototype sites have many pages that are viewed infrequently, a weighted sort type can be useful for focusing only on the highly visited pages that are more important to fix or reinforce.

If different landing or entry pages are used to distinguish between customer acquisition channels or campaigns, then the 'Landing Pages' report will reveal performance differences in terms of bounce rates and conversion rates based on initial entry. Linking acquisition to behavior is important for ensuring that a business prototype is not simply attracting visitors just to hit a customer acquisition goal but is targeting the right visitors that will be satisfied by the user experience.

The 'Site Speed' reports are useful for identifying pages that take too much time to load. While the average web page might take almost eight seconds to load, research suggests that visitors start to disappear when wait times go beyond three seconds, and that every extra second of delay might result in a 7% conversion rate reduction on average [4]. Google provides analysis tools that suggest ways of speeding up a page, both in Analytics and in the Google Search Console. More specific performance improvement suggestions are discussed in Chapter 13.

Conversion Report Analysis

A well-chosen conversion goal is the best indicator of digital business success. Everything else—the customer value proposition, the competitor positioning, the customer acquisition strategy, and the user experience— is all intended to produce a conversion as efficiently and effectively as possible.

The conversion rate for an appropriate goal is often the single best indicator of performance. Digital entrepreneurs should be carefully monitoring their conversion rate over time and comparing it to the current digital business design. The more analytics data is available, the more clues there will be about how to optimize conversion rates. Conversions by source [3] is one of the most popular reports for analysis, but 'Reverse Goal Path' and 'Goal Flow' reports are useful for visualizing which aspects of the business' user experience are creating conversions. Find the main paths to conversion, and try varying the content, appearance, or features on this path to make it even more effective. Segments can be used to separate the actions of visitors who convert from those who don't, or to separate different types of visitors with distinctive needs.

For online stores, conversion reports give a detailed look at the funnel, or the sequence of pages from investigation, to placing items in the cart, to checkout and payment. Add-ons for services such as WooCommerce or Shopify can automatically provide sales information to Google Analytics, providing data on not just numbers of conversions, but sales values. This data can be used to study the frequency of purchases, as well as average sales values. The digital entrepreneur can then try different content, appearance, or features on the prototype and see its effects on sales. This detailed e-commerce tracking also provides data on how many visits and interactions are required before a purchase is made, tracing the user experience across multiple sessions.

A/B Testing

If digital entrepreneurship can be thought of as a series of business experiments, then *A/B testing* is one of the most powerful tools for running experiments that will test and improve business ideas. In an A/B test, visitors are randomly sent to two different versions of a business prototype site. The version that successfully converts more visitors into customers is the better solution.

While digital entrepreneurs are always experimenting informally, by trying out new things on their prototypes and checking the analytics data, A/B testing is a real experimental design, similar to those used in scientific and medical research. With the right conversion goal and the right audience, this kind of testing tells entrepreneurs whether their ideas are actually causing an increase in business performance. The large technology platform companies, from Netflix and Amazon to Microsoft and Google, all run hundreds if not thousands of official experiments a week on their own customers [5]. Something as simple as the rearrangement of an image, or a slight change or highlighting of text, can increase conversion rates by 10–20% or more [6].

A/B testing can experiment with changing how a site looks, but ideas for testing are only limited by the entrepreneur's imagination. A good experiment is simple and inexpensive to conduct, will get answers quickly, and measures outcomes against a specific prediction or hypothesis [7].

Suggestions for A/B tests include:

- The location, size, or text of the call to action.

- The large 'hero' image on a page [3].

- The brand image or message for an entire site.

- The content of an important landing page.

- A different product image.

- The content of high bounce rate pages [8].

- A new product or service.

- A different kind of appeal, or testimonial.

- Different discounts, specials, giveaways, or price points. (A special discount can be offered to only a small number of randomly selected visitors.)

- A different final conversion page at the end of a multi-step shopping cart, registration, or other conversion process.

- The number or location of advertisements.

- Additional 'thank you' gifts or offers on a final confirmation page.

The preceding suggestions are practical ideas for A/B tests, but the overall objective is to make business ideas work better. Even as we madly experiment, we need to keep the bigger picture in mind for digital business success: motivating a customer; providing a clear, credible, and unique value proposition; being relevant for customer needs; providing an incentive or urgency for customer action; and all in an environment free of unnecessary distractions and anything that might create anxiety or friction [9].

All A/B tests include a hypothesis, or a prediction about what the effects of a change will be. For digital business prototypes, a hypothesis is that making a change from version A to version B will increase a conversion rate by some percentage. Entrepreneurs should prioritize the A/B testing experiments that have the potential to affect conversion rates the most, though it's sometimes difficult to know ahead of time which experiments have the most potential. Success as a digital entrepreneur depends on learning as efficiently as possible.

An extension of the A/B test, the multivariate test, randomly assigns visitors to more than one version of a site at the same time. A multivariate test can try a number of different changes at the same time, such as varying text placement, images, and content, and evaluate which of those changes has the most impact on conversion rates. Multivariate testing can speed up a series of experiments but requires more visitor traffic to find statistically meaningful differences [10]. With even more traffic, 'bandit' and other machine learning algorithms can be used to automatically steer more visitors to the most successful versions while an experiment is still taking place.

Implementing A/B Tests

For web sites, such as a digital business prototype, A/B testing works by adding a piece of code to each page. This code randomly sends visitors either to the original version of a page, or one or more other variants. Google Optimize is a popular tool for A/B testing that works well with Google Analytics, and has a feature-rich free version.

To start, create an account and a 'Container' at Google Optimize. A container needs to be created for each site to be tested, and each container will be linked to the site's property in Google Analytics. In the right column of the container administration screen, click on 'Link to Google Analytics', and copy and paste the property ID from Google Analytics.

Next, create a new experiment by clicking on the 'CREATE EXPERIMENT' button on the container administration screen. Give your experiment a name and copy and paste the URL of the page to be tested. A 'Redirect test' will randomly send visitors to two different versions of a page that you have already created. This is most useful when you need exact control over how the different A and B versions are designed, or if the changes are quite significant.

An 'A/B test' opens up an editor which allows you to make simple changes to a web page without having to create a new one. (The 'A/B test' editor only works in the Google Chrome browser, and requires the 'Google Optimize Extension' to be installed.) Save your new experiment.

Each experiment requires an objective, or a measurement which determines whether version B is better than version A. To test a business prototype, the best experimental objective is normally the main conversion goal that has been already defined in Google Analytics. Add the main conversion goal as the experimental objective and save.

The final step is to add the A/B testing code to the prototype site. Just like Google Analytics, Google Optimize code can be added to pages manually by copying and pasting tracking code by hand. The code can be found in the right column of the container administration page, at the 'INSTALL OPTIMIZE' link. Manual copying and pasting is useful when testing a single web page at a web building site, for example.

For those of us using a full WordPress prototype site, a plugin will automatically install Google Optimize code for us. In the WordPress administrator area, select 'Google Analytics' on the left, then 'Tracking Code', then the 'Integration' tab. Turn on 'enable Optimize tracking', copy and paste the container ID from Google Optimize, and save changes.

Back at Google Optimize, you are now ready to start the experiment. Once started, visitors should be randomly assigned to the different variants of your page. The reports at Google Optimize will say what the difference is in conversion rates, and whether there have been enough visitors, and if there is enough of a difference for a statistically significant change in conversion rate.

Congratulations! You have now taken the one of the biggest steps of all into digital business and digital entrepreneurship—the ability to experiment!

Google Analytics will also report on experimental results in the behavior reports under 'Experiments'.

The Google Analytics experiment reports will not just report experimental results, but also relate experimental behavior to other aspects of customer acquisition and behavior. Reporting can be broken down by segments, to see if experimental results work equally well for all kinds of users, or for all customer acquisition channels. Performance differences between segments can reveal opportunities to customize or personalize for particular audiences.

A/B testing is great on prototype sites but can also be useful for customer acquisition. A/B tests for customer acquisition can be implemented on many advertising and email marketing platforms, including the Google Ad Network and Facebook Ads. Two or more versions of an advertisement or a newsletter are created, and an advertising platform will automatically compare the click-through rates, or other conversion goals such as social media engagement, to see which performs the best. Different campaigns can be used to test the effectiveness of different customer acquisition activities by sending visitors to unique URLs and landing pages, but without randomly assigning visitors to one version or the other, they are not a true experimental design.

Updating the Digital Business Design: Improving, Pivoting, or Letting Go

Prototyping, experimenting, trying new things — these activities are all a good fit with the lean startup philosophy of entrepreneurship, where the early phases of entrepreneurship are all about searching for a viable business model. For this school of entrepreneurship, the best way to find the right business model is to learn as quickly and cheaply as possible. Fast learning becomes the main competitive advantage of the entrepreneur over existing businesses who have to overcome previous investments, the demands of existing customers, and the objections of internal stakeholders in order to try anything new.

While a lean startup doesn't have to be digital, the digital world makes this approach much more effective. As long as an entrepreneur is able to express their business idea in the form of a digital business design, it can be tested digitally and improved using data. Having a clear hypothesis or prediction about how a new business will perform is the most important tool for making the critical decision about whether to change aspects of the digital business design or not, which is known as a *pivot* in the lean startup philosophy.

Ries argues that almost every successful digital business startup has made at least one major pivot in its rise to stardom [11]. Certainly there are famous examples: YouTube starting as a dating service; Twitter as a side project at a podcasting company; or TripAdvisor as an expert travel review site that happened to add user comments. Beyond having clear performance goals to compare against, such as a regularly updated digital business design, there are few magic rules or research findings to help decide when an entrepreneur should consider pivoting in a new direction, versus trying to improve the business as currently designed [12].

Different types of pivot have been identified by Ries and others, including:

- *Feature pivot*—either expanding a feature, making a single feature the entire product; or shrinking a product to one of its features.

- *Customer needs pivot* — focusing on a new customer segment, or a new problem of interest to the same customer segment.

- *Platform pivot* — shifting from being a product to becoming a platform (such as to a community or matchmaker model); or shifting from being a platform for others to providing a product directly.

- *Revenue model pivot* — changing the main revenue model of the business.

- *Customer acquisition pivot* — using different channels or techniques to find new customers.

The fascinating thing about the digital business world is that the potential for pivoting along each of these dimensions is now much higher. While pivoting is never easy, it is at least possible.

The continuing job of the entrepreneur is to update the digital business design and the digital business prototype based on what is learned from experimentation, analytics data, user experience testing, and other forms of validation such as customer feedback surveys, online reviews, and direct conversations. Given the chance, reality can be a powerful voice in helping us decide how far to push a new business idea before we either find success or realize that our latest business hypothesis is just too far outside of our resources and interests to pursue further.

Everything that is learned about a new business idea is based on many assumptions and imperfect data. Making the assumptions as explicit as possible and testing them frequently are powerful skills for digital entrepreneurs. Staying close to the data by knowing exactly how it is produced is important. When data is collected at a distance, it can be difficult to know which parts are irrelevant or poor quality. The director of analytics for the National Basketball Association claims that 90% of their time is spent cleaning up data in spreadsheets for others to use [1]. Stay close to the business and the customer, try new things, and pore through the data that is generated based on your actions. Do this for long enough, and soon it will become worthwhile to launch a new digital business for real.

Additional Resources

https://searchengineland.com/7-essential-google-analytics-reports-every-marketer-must-know-250412 — guide to useful analytics reports.

https://conversionxl.com/blog/12-google-analytics-custom-reports/ — examples of custom analytics reports, and the questions they can answer.

https://ga-dev-tools.appspot.com/campaign-url-builder/ — custom URL building tool for campaigns.

www.optimizely.com/optimization-glossary/ab-testing/ — A/B testing explanation and examples.

https://conversionxl.com/blog/ab-testing-guide/ — more A/B testing examples, including multivariate, and bandit testing.

http://firstround.com/review/the-tenets-of-a-b-testing-from-duolingos-master-growth-hacker/ — case study of A/B testing at Duolingo.

www.designforfounders.com/ab-testing-examples/ — more A/B testing examples.

https://optinmonster.com/8-ab-tests-to-run-on-your-popups-to-get-more-email-subscribers/ — tips for specific A/B tests.

https://marketingplatform.google.com/about/resources/the-motley-fool-increases-order-page-conversion-rate-optimize-360/ — case study using Google Optimize to increase email conversion rate.

Exercises

12.1.   Identify two pages on a digital business prototype site that would benefit the most from A/B testing. For each page, how would you vary the content between the two versions, and why?

12.2.   Run an A/B experiment on a prototype site for at least 50 visitors. Describe the results of your experiment, particularly with respect to conversion rates.

12.3.   Compare the customer acquisition data for a prototype site to its customer acquisition goals. For each channel, discuss whether action is necessary to improve customer acquisition performance.

12.4.   Compare the bounce rate on a prototype site to industry norms. Discuss whether actions need to be taken to improve bounce rate.

12.5.   Identify the most common path visitors take through a prototype site. From the initial entry to site exit, discuss the most important issues for user experience that need improvement.

12.6.   Create a two-week plan for the most important experiments to be conducted on a prototype site in the areas of customer acquisition, user experience, and conversions. Implement the plan.

12.7.   Using at least a week of analytics data, compare the results to the conversion equation for a prototype site. Discuss the main lessons you draw from these results.

12.8.   At the end of the experimental period, discuss the advantages and disadvantages of continuing to pursue the original business idea, pivoting, or terminating the project.

References

[1]   F. Alhlou, S. Asif, and E. Fettman, *Google Analytics Breakthrough: From Zero to Business Impact*. Hoboken, NJ: John Wiley & Sons, 2016.

[2]   J. Peyton. *Good, Bad, Ugly, and Average Bounce Rates*. (2014), available: www.gorocketfuel.com/the-rocket-blog/whats-the-average-bounce-rate-in-google-analytics/. [Accessed: August 20, 2018].

[3]   A. Kaushik, *Web Analytics 2.0: The Art of Online Accountability and Science of Customer Centricity*. Indianapolis: Wiley Publishing, 2011.

[4]   Machmetrics.com. *Average Page Load Times for 2018—How Does Yours Compare?* (2018), available: www.machmetrics.com/speed-blog/average-page-load-times-websites-2018/. [Accessed: August 21, 2018].

[5]   R. Kohavi and S. Thomke, "The Surprising Power of Online Experiments," *Harvard Business Review*, vol. 95, no. 5, pp. 74–82, 2017.

[6]   G. Krishnan. *Selecting the Best Artwork for Videos through a/B Testing*. (2016), available: https://medium.com/netflix-techblog/selecting-the-best-artwork-for-videos-through-a-b-testing-f6155c4595f6. [Accessed: August 21, 2018].

[7]   A. Ganguly and J. Euchner, "Conducting Business Experiments: Validating New Business Models Well-Designed Business Experiments Can Help Validate Assumptions and Reduce Risk Associated with New Business Models," *Research-Technology Management*, vol. 61, no. 2, pp. 27–36, 2018.

[8]   B. Clifton, *Advanced Web Metrics with Google Analytics*. Indianapolis, Indiana: John Wiley & Sons, 2012.

[9]   D. Croxen-John and J. van Tonder, *E-Commerce Website Optimization: Why 95 Per Cent of Your Webiste Visitors Don't Buy and What You Can Do About It*. London: Kogan Page, 2017.

[10]   optimizely.com. *Multivariate Testing Vs a/B Testing*. (2018), available: www.optimizely.com/optimization-

glossary/multivariate-test-vs-ab-test/. [Accessed: August 21, 2018].

[11]   E. Ries, *The Lean Startup: How Today's Entrepreneurs Use Continuous Innovation to Create Radically Successful Businesses*. New York: Crown Business, 2011.

[12]   J. Bosch, H. H. Olsson, J. Björk, and J. Ljungblad, "The Early Stage Software Startup Development Model: A Framework for Operationalizing Lean Principles in Software Startups," in *Lean Enterprise Software and Systems*: Springer, 2013, pp. 1–15.

Launching a New Digital Business Venture

Highlights

Chapter 13 discusses four of the major issues faced by new digital businesses as they open their virtual doors to the world: legal and regulatory compliance, security and disaster recovery, technical performance, and custom development.

- Basic legal protections, such as terms of service and clear privacy policies, reduce the likelihood of legal problems. Intellectual property law, particularly copyright and trademark, are important issues for site content creation, user contributions, and domain name selection.

- Cybersecurity has become a critical risk for any digital business. No site can ever be completely secure, so the goal of security is to focus on the simplest, most effective means of improving security, while at the same time being prepared to restore from backup if an attack or ransom attempt causes irreparable harm.

- If the technical performance of a digital business site starts affecting customer behavior, there are ways to improve performance and options for more powerful deployment technologies as customer numbers grow.

- Digital entrepreneurs can seek out custom development of new add-ons, code, and mobile apps as business needs become more complex.

Launching a New Digital Business

With the heavy use of Minimum Viable Products (MVPs) and experimentation, the boundary can sometimes be unclear between an early business experiment and the official launch of a new digital business. Digital businesses signal this by labeling their products as early, unfinished prototypes, calling them 'alpha' releases or 'beta' releases [1], and sometimes closing the initial set of customers to those recruited by invitation only. Some digital products are kept in a kind of 'perpetual beta', as Google's Gmail product was for many years [2]. Eventually, with enough customers, and enough revenue or value being created, it is time to make a new digital business official.

A new digital business shares many of the same concerns as any startup in the physical world, including: assembling the right team, naming a business, deciding on ownership structure, paying taxes, hiring employees, keeping the books, raising money, building a brand, and promoting the business through offline channels. These traditional startup topics are well covered in existing guides [3]. The focus of this chapter is on four important topics where digital business startups face unique challenges and risks as they reach out to the wider world: legal issues, cybersecurity, technical performance and operations, and custom development.

Legal Issues

As soon as a new business begins to work with real customers or investors, legal issues should be on the mind of a digital entrepreneur. The discussion in this section raises relevant issues but is not written by lawyers and is not legal advice. The first two specialists any entrepreneur should hire are a good lawyer and a good accountant [3]. In consultation with legal professionals, consider taking action in the following areas:

- Adding terms of service.

- Adding a privacy policy and implementing compliance with new European Union GDPR privacy regulations.

- Implement an intellectual property strategy, particularly for copyright and trademarks.

- Compliance with e-commerce and online selling laws, especially for online stores.

Terms of Service: Every digital business site should have a *terms of service* page. Though few people read them when signing up for a new service [4], they provide basic and necessary legal protections for the business. Free online templates and generators can be used as a starting point for building a terms of service page, as can the terms of service used by other similar sites. The use of some technologies requires additional language in a terms of service. For example, the Google Analytics terms of service requires notifying users that they are being tracked, and if demographics and interest information is being collected and used.

A basic terms of service document includes standard information about user rights and responsibilities, references to privacy and copyright policy, and disclaimers of liability. In the US context, it should be explicitly stated that unauthorized or illegal uses are prohibited. Special rules and regulations apply in the US if children under the age of 13 are allowed to use the site. If users are allowed to make comments and/or upload content, it can be helpful to have explicit policies for dealing with complaints and removing libelous or offensive material. Consider including a disclaimer that the business is not responsible for the accuracy or reliability of third-party statements [5].

Privacy Policy: Digital businesses that collect and use personally identifiable information are required by law in most jurisdictions to publish a *privacy policy*. In the US, the California Online Privacy Protection Act (CalOPPA) provides a standard baseline [6]. CalOPPA requires sites to have a prominent link to a privacy policy. A CalOPPA complaint policy includes:

- What types of personal information are collected, including browser cookies.

- How personal information may be shared with others.

- How users can see and edit their personal information.

- How the business responds to 'Do Not Track' requests from browsers.

- When and how the policy has changed over time.

Additional specialized requirements apply in the US at the federal level for specialized situations such as health care information (HIPPA), financial information, and for users under the age of 13 (COPPA). California has an additional 'Online Eraser' law that requires a mechanism for users under age 18 to delete all information and content they have posted on a site.

Many digital businesses around the world are making their privacy policies even stronger by conforming to the new European Union Data Protection Regulation (GDPR) [7]. GDPR privacy policy requirements include:

- Users must explicitly opt in to the privacy policy (not just have an available link to look at).

- Personally identifiable information should be collected for specific uses only. Users must be told why it is being collected and how long it is kept.

- Users being informed of their right to access data about themselves and to have their personal data removed (the 'right to be forgotten').

- Informing users of security breaches that expose their personal information.

- If information is sent outside the EU, specifying which countries are processing their information, and their level of data protection.

In certain circumstances, a digital business will need to appoint an independent Data Protection Officer (DPO) to monitor compliance with the GDPR. For example, Germany requires every organization with more than ten employees to establish a DPO [8]. For sites that use web analytics services such as Google Analytics, users need to be informed of the exact information being collected and be offered an opportunity to opt out of tracking. Some personal information such as exact IP addresses may need to be removed. Google Analytics provides additional language to include in a privacy policy and is making tools available that allow individual users to delete their data more easily [9].

For WordPress sites, newly created sites now include a draft privacy policy. New capabilities under the 'Tools' menu include the ability to export or delete information for individual users. Plugins are available for obtaining permission to use cookies, which is now required by the GDPR, and for adding opt-in checkboxes to contact forms and other requests for personally identifiable information.

Intellectual Property: Two immediate intellectual property concerns for new digital businesses are trademarks and copyright. A *trademark* is a name, phrase, or symbol that identifies the source of a product or service in a marketplace. Trademarks that are similar enough to be confused by consumers with other businesses that sell similar products and services create a legal risk [10]. In the US, trademarks do not have to be registered, but registration makes legal enforcement actions easier, especially at the national or international level [5]. A trademark can also be applied for at the global level through the WIPO.

The main trademark issue for new digital businesses is the domain name [11]. Domain names that infringe upon an existing trademark are subject to anti-cybersquatting laws in the US. Though the likelihood of legal trouble might be low for a new digital business with little visibility, a trademark search on a proposed domain name at the USPTO database is a good idea. Be careful using the trademarks of other companies in site content without acknowledging their ownership. Parody site domain names are legally protected in the US ('walmartsucks. org') but be prepared for legal wrangling if it catches their attention.

Thinking ahead to future domain names that can be successfully registered as trademarks, names that are either totally invented (for example, 'fiverr') or have no meaningful connection with a product or service (for example, 'Rainbows and Unicorns Consulting', unless your consulting business is about rainbows and unicorns) are the safest, while generic terms and words that describe the product or service are the most difficult to trademark.

A *copyright* protects original works of authorship by giving the author exclusive rights to use and sell the content they create. As soon as a work is produced in fixed and tangible form, including publishing on a web page, copyright protections apply. In the US, copyright registration is not required for protection, though some digital businesses put language at the bottom of their pages claiming their copyright. Reciprocal copyright protections exist between most developed countries.

Because a copyright is essentially a restriction on how others may copy and use original content, some businesses prefer to share their content more widely by relaxing or giving up copyright protections. Original content can be placed in the public domain for all to use without restriction. Or authors can use creative commons licenses to put some restrictions on reuse but allow more kinds of sharing which may get their content more visibility.

Creative commons licenses can restrict content to non-commercial uses only, allow or restrict changes, or simply insist that the original authors are given credit without in any way restricting their use [12]. One of their most interesting licenses is the 'ShareAlike', which is similar to the software license used by WordPress and other open source software. This license lets people use and modify content freely but requires that any changes or improvements must be shared with the world using the same license. This copyright breakthrough has made openness a fundamental part of our digital world.

Digital businesses that are community based, or accept user uploads, have to pay attention to the issue of copyright violations by their users. In the US context, sites are protected from copyright violations by their users in certain circumstances by the Digital Millennium Copyright Act (DMCA). According to the DMCA, sites are generally not held responsible for the copyright violations of their users, as long as a site clearly designates an agent who can accept 'takedown notices', or official requests by copyright owners to remove offending content, and those requests are responded to promptly [13]. This 'safe harbor' protection is a lifesaver for community-based businesses but be sure to make the notification process for copyright violations clear and consistent with the DMCA.

E-commerce Law: Any business that buys or sells goods online is subject to e-commerce laws in the jurisdictions where transactions take place. In the US context, the Federal Trade Commission (FTC) requires business to have clear policies for shipping, returns, and any warranties or guarantees. Products that are offered for sale should be real—purchases must normally be shipped within 30 days [5]. US states can have more specific regulations. For example, California law states that if a return policy isn't posted, customers are entitled to a full refund within 30 days. In the US, truth in advertising laws require all business not to make false or misleading claims about their product, or to publish advertisements that make false or misleading claims.

Other examples of relevant e-commerce law in the US context include [14]:

- *Revealing paid endorsements or incentives*—bloggers and others who endorse products must disclose any gifts or incentives they receive for recommending the product, including affiliate marketing links, according to FTC Guidelines. The disclosure must be visible from the endorsement or purchase link, not in a separate 'About Us' or 'Terms of Service' page.

- *Opting out of marketing messages*—the CAN-SPAM act requires all electronic communications with commercial messages, including marketing emails, to provide a means of opting out of future communications. The message must also have a valid physical mail address, and the subject line of the message must reflect the content accurately.

- *Free speech in consumer reviews* — the Consumer Review Fairness Act prohibits businesses from including in their terms of service any language that would prohibit consumers from leaving an honest and truthful review of their business, even if it is negative. Consumers also retain the intellectual property rights to any reviews posted.

European Union e-commerce law includes requirements for making purchasing terms clear. All website purchases must be confirmed within 24 hours, and customers must be informed of their right to withdraw from any contracts within a 14-day period [15]. EU law also requires a posted cookie policy, in addition to its data protection policies under the GDPR as discussed above.

The legal issues associated with starting any new business should be addressed with the help of legal professionals. Legal issues mentioned here are meant to be helpful for planning and discussion purposes and are not a substitute for real legal advice.

Security and Disaster Recovery

Cybersecurity has become a critical risk that every digital business must manage. No site can ever be completely secure, so the goal of security in the early phases of a new business is to focus on the simplest, most effective means of improving security, while at the same time being prepared to restore an up-to-date copy of a digital business site elsewhere if an attack or ransom attempt causes irreparable harm.

For business prototypes built with freely available software such as WordPress, the most important cybersecurity activities include regular software updates, access control and monitoring, and site backups. Security plugins are available that look for common security problems and make recommendations for fixes.

Regular Software Updates: Because of the popularity of WordPress software, WordPress sites are frequently the target of automated hacking attempts [16]. Attackers try to log on, gain access to, or modify thousands of sites with simple attacks, hoping to find a site with an obvious or fairly basic security problem. The popularity of WordPress software also means, however, that a large community is on the lookout for bugs or errors that can be exploited by hackers and is creating fixes for those bugs.

Perhaps the single most important security protection is to regularly update a site's software. If the core WordPress software is not updated regularly, hackers can take advantage of known security problems with older versions. Fortunately, WordPress now automatically updates its core software. However, there can be serious security problems with any plugin or theme, as these also contain software code that might have errors. Keep plugins and themes regularly updated as well. While the ability to add code to a WordPress site easily is a big part of its appeal, this division or *modularity* of software can cause problems when a software update in one part of the code causes it to no longer work with other software that has not been updated. Update headaches are yet another reason to stick with plugins and themes that are active and regularly updated.

Access Control and Monitoring: Denying unauthorized access to your new business is important. It is an eye-opening experience to see how many unauthorized users try to log into even the smallest digital business every day or try to enter some kind of malicious information into forms or comments. Popular methods of access control include:

- Using strong passwords and non-standard account names (not 'admin') and requiring password changes on a regular basis.

- Monitoring login attempts, and limiting failed login attempts to a small number using a plugin. This will prevent most attempts to login with commonly used passwords.

- Using a firewall, either at the hosting service or with a security plugin, to block access attempts from particular IP addresses that are repeated sources of break-in attempts.

- Using SSL certificates and the 'https://' version of site URLs. While this is more of a tool for authentication, ensuring that users are not sent to a fake version of a business, it prevents a common attack that hackers use to obtain login information from unsuspecting users. Most web hosting will now include an SSL certificate by default.

Site Backups: If hackers do succeed at breaking into a business and infect it with malware or otherwise deny you access to your own business, having a current backup copy of your site and the ability to reinstall it will allow your business to get up and running again quickly. For a site made up of web pages, the pages themselves can be backed up in the cloud, or a usb drive, and later copied to a new server or web hosting account. Your business' domain name can then be pointed to the nameservers for the hosting service at the new location.

For WordPress sites, a full backup includes hundreds of files: web pages, added themes, added plugins, media files, and user uploads. A WordPress site also includes a database which stores page and post content, user accounts, and other tables with information about the site. A good backup plugin such as 'UpdraftPlus' will automatically store all files and a copy of the database to a remote location. But just as importantly, a good plugin will easily reinstall the saved site at a new location.

Any entrepreneur who owns a digital business needs to be able to reinstall a backup copy of their site or hire someone who can. Rule number one is not to simply make site backups and hope that, when the time comes, the backup can be reinstalled. Practice reinstalling a backup before disaster strikes.

Technical Performance

As visitor numbers grow from the hundreds to the thousands, tens of thousands, and beyond, the performance of digital business sites can degrade to the point where potential customers are discouraged and disappear. Every extra second of page loading time increases the chances of a bounce and lowers the conversion rate.

A good first step is to evaluate the performance of your digital business. Loading speed problems are easily found by using the site, but the 'Site Speed' reports under 'BEHAVIOR' in Google Analytics provide more systematic data about which pages are the slowest. The 'Overview' report breaks down loading times into server connection and response times, and page download times. Server problems are addressed through your shared hosting provider, or by switching to a more powerful (and expensive) server technology. Page loading problems are more under your own control.

Web pages with many high-resolution images, and with many pieces of code that call other software services, are often the slowest. Large images can be resized to a lower resolution using freely available photo editing tools with little or no visual difference on typical screens. If many high-resolution images or files are needed, a specialized Content Distribution Network (CDN) can be used to speed up content delivery to users all over the world [17].

Sites built using WordPress and other content management software can be slow because each page is dynamically generated. A dynamic web page must be created by running software code and retrieving information from databases every time a user asks for it. To speed up response times, a page can be copied into a cache after it is generated. A cache is a short-term storage area. If the page has not changed since the last time it was asked for, the copy of the finished page can be sent without generating it again. Caching can make page speeds two, three, or even ten times faster. WordPress plugins such as 'W3 Total Cache' and 'WP Super Cache' are easy to install and activate.

After taking these steps, if performance still isn't fast enough, it may be time to upgrade the server technology. The shared hosting technology we have used for prototyping is cheap and relatively user friendly, but it is not high performance. Once a digital business goes beyond a few thousand monthly visitors, simultaneous user requests can really slow down a shared server, especially when the server is being shared with 50 or 100 other sites.

The next level up in performance is Virtual Private Server (VPS) web hosting. A VPS service shares a server with fewer other sites, speeding up performance [18]. An advantage is that many shared hosting services offer an easy migration path to a VPS upgrade, taking care of many of the installation details. A downside is that VPS hosting often assumes that the account owner is comfortable with command lines and basic systems administration tasks. It is rewarding to learn some of this yourself, but with thousands of customers it could be time to call in some systems administration help. The next level up would be a dedicated server, devoted only to your business. Moving up to hundreds of thousands of users a month, a systems architect would connect additional servers that specialize in particular tasks: a load balancer to distribute requests among multiple web servers, along with specialized database servers.

A different pathway for server growth taken by many high-growth technology startups is to use cloud-based services. With cloud services, servers can be rented by the minute or hour, dynamically adjusting server capacity depending on demand. Amazon Web Services is the pioneer in this market, but other major players such as Microsoft and Google also offer the equivalent of a year's worth of free server time to new users. Cloud services have become easier to use over time, especially with the addition of cloud VPS services such as Amazon Lightsail. Setting up cloud services still involves a bit of command line work, so it hasn't been featured in this book for the non-technologist. We expect that within the next few years, cloud VPS services will become easy enough to use for entrepreneurial prototyping, even for beginners.

Custom and Mobile Development

The technology that entrepreneurs with no coding experience can use to prototype a new digital business is truly incredible. Simple services such as shared web hosting and freely available software code such as WordPress allow beginners to create a sophisticated online presence. However, at some point, existing plugins and themes may not be enough. More complex automation, more sophisticated use of data, more sophisticated interfaces to other services such as machine learning, or the making of an iOS or Android mobile app all require custom coding. At this stage, it is time for the entrepreneur to either learn some coding on their own, bring in a technical partner, or explore hiring a freelancer for custom software development.

Mobile apps are often first on the custom development wish list. A WordPress prototype site uses standard web technologies such as responsive CSS to automatically adjust a user interface to different screen sizes, providing a mobile experience that feels somewhat like a native mobile app. Responsive mobile web sites may need additional customization but can provide a surprisingly good mobile device experience [19]. Mobile web sites are sometimes easier to find and start using than mobile apps because they don't require an app store download. A site optimized for mobile will also improve its search rankings [20].

The advantages of a true mobile app, if it is downloaded by a potential customer, are that it is likely be used more often and can take advantage of more information, features, and gestures available on a user's phone. Native mobile apps must be coded in either the Swift language for Apple iOS or the variant of Java used on Android devices. Services exist for converting an existing WordPress site into a mobile app; they are fairly basic, but if an instant mobile app is a must they can be useful.

A typical mobile app, however, will require custom coding. Software development skills can be recruited to the team via employment or an equity stake, but there is competition for development talent. Or entrepreneurs can take advantage of freelancers. Many online marketplaces offer freelance technical services. General purpose sites such as Upwork allow entrepreneurs to search for freelancers themselves and make bids for projects. Services such as Toptal try to match a general description of the work needed with an appropriate freelancer. Some freelance sites are specific to particular technologies or platforms, such as Codeable.io for custom WordPress development.

In the search for a freelancer, look at their portfolio and testimonials from previous projects that are similar to yours [21]. Research their reputation and reviews beyond the freelancer site they are listed on. Some entrepreneurs will do a brief interview with technology specific questions, or if there's time engage a freelancer on a small test project first.

Before engaging a freelancer, it helps to be familiar with the basics of contract law and project management. Get everything in writing [22]. Be as specific as you can about the technical requirements of the project and try to anticipate problems before they arise [5]. Additional considerations for freelancer contracts include:

- Transferring ownership of any work to you, the entrepreneur. Make it clear that the work is 'made for hire' so that you own the intellectual property.

- Do not pay up front all at once. Have milestones and phase the payments. Include termination provisions that will cancel the contract if certain conditions are not met.

- Specify the project in as much objective detail as possible. Try to divide into smaller projects to keep the scope focused.

- Agree on what maintenance the freelancer is willing to do, if any.

The more an entrepreneur understands about the details of their own business and technology, the better their project management skills will be. If an entrepreneur or someone on their team cannot evaluate the technical quality of the work, it will be difficult to manage freelance work effectively.

Our Final Milestone: Launch

Congratulations on making it here! This has been a whirlwind tour of the digital entrepreneurship world. We have only barely scratched the surface of what it possible. Each one of the chapter topics could be a whole course by itself, or a whole career specialization. There are so many ways to develop your digital entrepreneurship skills further from here:

- Design: Learning more about how to generate great digital business ideas, find new customer needs, and how to turn ideas into specific design for testing.

- Coding: Getting stronger at building prototypes and apps by learning web design and new programming languages.

- UX: Learning more about UX—user experience, usability testing, use cases, and customer journeys.

- Analytics: Becoming an expert at web analytics analysis and implementation.

- Digital marketing: Building skills in customer acquisition and digital marketing—including search optimization, social media marketing, paid advertising campaigns, and email marketing.

- Expertise: Becoming an expert in a particular product market or subject area and translating that expertise into digital content that builds a professional reputation.

Hopefully, the act of launching your first digital business, even a small one, will make it clear how all these pieces fit together and give you enough of a taste to figure out what your next steps should be.

Don't worry if your first attempt at digital entrepreneurship isn't a billion-dollar unicorn. The entrepreneurial skills you learn are more important than your first project. Entrepreneurs are different than most other people in the way they embrace failure as a learning experience and as a natural part of risk taking.

In any new digital venture you launch, always have clear goals and performance expectations. Get a specific 'ABC' process up and running and know how it's doing. Constantly explore new products and services, new customer acquisition strategies, new user experiences, new revenue models, and new conversion goals, but always be able to compare them to what came before. Extreme experimentation and change, based on unique data, with an ability to scale up and down easily, is the new digital business reality. You can now be a part of it.

One last thing: If you find this kind of digital entrepreneurship at all interesting or useful, take a part of what you have learned and share it with someone else. For entrepreneurship and innovation to be truly inclusive in the new digital era, more people need to believe that they too can become digital entrepreneurs. The digital future should be for the many, not the few. Good luck to ya!

Additional Resources

https://termsfeed.com/blog/sample-terms-of-service-template/—terms of service template.
https://termsfeed.com/blog/sample-privacy-policy-template/—privacy policy template.

www.rocketlawyer.com/sem/website-terms-of-use.rl — terms of service generator for US-based businesses, a paid service but with free trial.

http://tess2.uspto.gov/ — online US trademark search.

https://wordpress.org/plugins/updraftplus/ — leading backup and recovery plugin for WordPress sites.

https://wordpress.org/plugins/w3-total-cache/ — leading caching plugin for WordPress.

https://aws.amazon.com/lightsail/ — cloud-based VPS hosting.

https://premium.wpmudev.org/blog/wordpress-site-mobile-app/ — services for automatically creating a mobile app from a WordPress site.

https://codeable.io/ — WordPress freelance developer marketplace.

Exercises

13.1.   Create a terms of service page and a privacy policy page for a digital business prototype site.

13.2.   Design a process for accepting intellectual property questions or complaints for your digital business. On the business prototype site, implement a means of contacting the person responsible for your intellectual property process.

13.3.   Discuss whether any conflict of interest or other disclosures are required on your prototype site. Implement any needed disclosures.

13.4.   Identify any barriers to automatic software updates on your digital business site, such as customizations, themes, or plugin compatibility. Describe how you will mitigate these concerns.

13.5.   Identify the two most important actions to be taken on your digital business site for reducing unauthorized access to your digital business.

13.6. Backup and restore your digital business site to another location.

13.7. Evaluate whether the performance of your digital business site is currently adequate.

13.8. Identify the two most important changes that will improve the performance of your digital business site. Implement those changes.

13.9. Estimate the number of visitors to your digital business site that will require a switch to different server technology. Find the monthly cost of that technology upgrade and discuss any barriers to making the transition.

13.10. Evaluate the quality of the mobile experience on your digital business site. Discuss whether any further actions to improve the mobile experience are required.

13.11. Create a proposal for a custom development or design project that will improve your digital business. Find at least two service providers online that might be appropriate for your project and estimate the time and cost.

13.12. Discuss whether your digital business would benefit from having a technical partner as a co-founder or employee. If so, discuss how easy or difficult it will be to find a suitable partner and how much of an equity stake might be required to attract their interest.

13.13. Present your completed digital business prototype, along with the digital business design and lessons learned from data and experimentation, to an investor or other person with experience in digital business. What is their feedback about next steps for the business?

References

[1]   J. Lee. *What Does "Beta Software" Really Mean?* (2013), available: www.makeuseof.com/tag/what-does-beta-software-really-mean/. [Accessed: August 25, 2018].

[2]   J. Lapidos. *Why Did It Take Google So Long to Take Gmail out of "Beta"?* (2009), available: www.slate.com/articles/news_and_politics/recycled/2009/07/why_did_it_take_google_so_long_to_take_gmail_out_of_beta.html. [Accessed: August 25, 2018].

[3]   Entrepreneur Media Inc., *Start Your Own Business: The Only Startup Book You'll Ever Need*, 7th ed. Irvine, CA: Entrepreneur Press, 2018.

[4]   J. A. Obar and A. Oeldorf-Hirsch, "The Biggest Lie on the Internet: Ignoring the Privacy Policies and Terms of Service Policies of Social Networking Services," *Information, Communication & Society*, pp. 1–20, (2018), available: https://www.tandfonline.com/loi/rics20

[5]   R. Stim and L. Guerin, *Running a Side Business: How to Create a Second Income*. Berkeley, CA: Nolo, 2009.

[6]   L. Hamilton. *Caloppa: California Online Privacy Protection Act.* (2018), available: https://termsfeed.com/blog/caloppa/. [Accessed: August 26, 2018].

[7]   L. Hamilton. *Gdpr: Eu General Data Protection Regulation.* (2018), available: https://termsfeed.com/blog/gdpr/. [Accessed: August 26, 2018].

[8]   itgovernance.co.uk. *The Dpo (Data Protection Officer) Role under the Gdpr.* (2018), available: www.itgovernance.co.uk/data-protection-officer-dpo-under-the-gdpr. [Accessed: August 25, 2018].

[9]   F. Alhlou, S. Asif, and E. Fettman, *Google Analytics Breakthrough: From Zero to Business Impact*. Hoboken, NJ: John Wiley & Sons, 2016.

[10]   United States *Patent* and Trademark Office. *Basic Facts About Trademarks.* (2016), available: www.uspto.gov/sites/default/files/BasicFacts.pdf.

[11]   nolo.com. *Avoid Trademark Infringement When You Choose a Domain Name.* (2018), available: www.nolo.com/legal-encyclopedia/avoid-trademark-infringement-domain-name-29032.html. [Accessed: August 27, 2018].

[12]   creativecommons.*org*. *About the Licenses*. (2017),
        available: https://creativecommons.org/licenses/.
        [Accessed: August 28, 2017].

[13]   United States *Copyright* Office. *Dmca Designated
        Agent Directory*. (2018), available: www.copyright.gov/
        dmca-directory/. [Accessed: August 27, 2018].

[14]   Federal Trade *Commission*. *Online Advertising and
        Marketing*. (2018), available: www.ftc.gov/tips-advice/
        business-center/advertising-and-marketing/online-
        advertising-and-marketing. [Accessed: August 28,
        2018].

[15]   European *Commission*. *Legal Regulations for
        E-Commerce*. (2018), available: https://ec.europa.eu/
        growth/sectors/tourism/business-portal/understanding-
        legislation/legal-regulations-e-commerce_en.
        [Accessed: August 28, 2017].

[16]   B. Barron. *Do You Know Why Hackers Are Targeting
        Your Wordpress Site?* (2018), available: https://
        premium.wpmudev.org/blog/do-you-know-why-
        hackers-are-targeting-your-wordpress-site/. [Accessed:
        August 30, 2018].

[17]   B. Jackson. *Wordpress Cdn—Why You Should Be
        Using One in 2018*. (2018), available: https://kinsta.com/
        blog/wordpress-cdn/. [Accessed: August 31, 2018].

[18]   J. Wilson. *The Best Vps Web Hosting Services
        of 2018*. (2018), available: www.pcmag.com/
        article2/0,2817,2455706,00.asp. [Accessed: August 31,
        2018].

[19]   T. Agrimbau. *Developing Mobile Web Applications:
        When, Why, and How*. (2018), available: www.toptal.
        com/android/developing-mobile-web-apps-when-why-
        and-how. [Accessed: August 31, 2018].

[20]   D. Ryan, Understanding *Digital Marketing: Marketing
        Strategies for Engaging the Digital Generation*. London:
        Kogan Page Publishers, 2016.

[21]   S. Belew and J. Elad, *Starting an Online Business All-
        in-One for Dummies*. Hoboken, NJ: John Wiley & Sons,
        2017.

[22]   J. Thomas. *3 Legal Precautions in Hiring Freelancers*.
        (2014), available: www.entrepreneur.com/article/
        235155. [Accessed: August 31, 2018].

Key Terms

A/B TESTING—a simple form of content experiment, where visitors are randomly assigned to two variants of a prototype, A and B, and their performance is compared on some measure. Multivariate testing uses more than two variants in the experiment.

ABC PROCESS—the basic process of digital business design that attracts and satisfies potential customers, leading to a successful action that has business value; an abbreviation for customer Acquisition, customer Behavior, and Conversion.

ACQUISITION—the attraction of online customers to a digital business through one or more channels; the first step in the ABC process of digital business.

ADD-ONS—code available to be added to software platforms that provide new features or functions; also known as plugins or modules.

BACK-END FEATURES—software features that affect operations behind the scenes and are not normally visible from the user interface.

BEHAVIOR—actions taken by visitors at an online presence such as a web page or app; the second step in the ABC process of digital business.

BUSINESS MODEL—a short description of the basic components of a digital business, including the value proposition for customers and other key contributors, the resources required to fulfill the value proposition, and how those resources will be obtained.

CHANNEL—a source of online visitor traffic; search and social media are two of the most commonly used channels in digital business.

COMMUNITY BUSINESS—type of digital business that creates customer value through specialized content and conversations, which are contributed mostly by users.

CONCIERGE MVP—a Minimum Viable Product prototype implemented through manual activities behind the scenes before a full digital site or app is built.

CONTENT BUSINESS—type of digital business that creates customer value through specialized content authored or acquired by the business.

CONTENT MANAGEMENT SOFTWARE—software for easily managing and updating content-based web sites; the majority of web sites in the world now use content management software.

CONTENT STRATEGY—strategy for producing and maintaining the content for a digital business, including content creation, delivery, and maintenance.

CONVERSION—action taken by a visitor that creates value for a digital business and defines a successful visit.

CONVERSION EQUATION—target number of conversions per time period a digital business is trying to achieve; normally expressed as the number of visitors per month times a conversion rate.

CONVERSION GOALS—specific, measurable digital actions that reflect a conversion; examples include a 'buy now' button click, an advertisement click, or a 'submit contact form' button click.

CONVERSION RATE—percentage of conversions per time period; a measure of the effectiveness of the ABC process.

DIGITAL BUSINESS—a business that is created digitally, and whose activities are predominantly conducted by digital means.

DIGITAL BUSINESS DESIGN—a high level overview of the main aspects of a digital business, structured around the ABC process.

DIGITAL ENTREPRENEURSHIP—entrepreneurship that is affected by, or takes advantage of, the digital transformation of business and society.

DISASTER RECOVERY—ability to restart a digital business from backups, in case of loss or security breach.

DOMAIN NAME—an easier to remember name for an internet resources and services registered with the Domain Name System (DNS); examples include twitter.com and jpedia.org.

ENGAGEMENT STRATEGY—part of social media strategy that identifies the content and community interaction intended to encourage social behaviors such as liking, sharing, commenting, and reviewing.

FRONT-END FEATURES—software features that affect the user interface and customer interactions.

INDIRECT REVENUE MODEL—a revenue model where the digital business itself does not earn money but creates actions that will lead to revenue later or somewhere else; examples include generating sales leads and information requests.

INFLUENCER STRATEGY—part of social media strategy that identifies and attracts well-connected influencers.

INTEGRATION FEATURES—software features that allow a web site or app to connect to other Internet services.

MATCHMAKING BUSINESS—type of digital business that creates value for the customer by bringing together otherwise disconnected sets of people.

MVP—abbreviation for Minimum Viable Product; a prototype with the minimum functionality and content required to test whether a digital business design makes sense. The prototype is deliberately kept simple in order to speed up learning and avoid overinvestment in digital business designs that are not viable.

NAVIGATION STRUCTURE—organization of menus and other visual features that help visitors find the right content and functionality easily.

PRIVACY POLICY—published statement of what personally identifiable information is collected by a digital business and how it is used, shared and kept. Normally includes procedures for dealing with privacy requests and complaints.

PROMOTION BUSINESS—type of digital business that creates value for an existing business by attracting customers.

PROTOTYPE—an online presence such as a web page, a web site, or a mobile app, used to test a digital business design.

REVENUE MODEL—means of generating revenue for a digital business; examples include sales, transaction fees, advertising, and donations.

SCREEN LAYOUT—a standard format for how content is displayed on a web site, often defined by a template or theme.

SEARCH RESULTS—the most relevant sites returned for a search query, the specific phrase entered into a search engine.

SEARCH ENGINE OPTIMIZATION—strategy and actions taken to improve search engine results for a particular keyword or keywords.

SEARCH KEYWORDS—words used by potential customers to find your digital business through a search engine.

STYLE SHEET—document with rules written in CSS (Cascading Style Sheet) language that specify the look and feel of a web page.

TERMS OF SERVICE—published document that specifies legitimate access and use of a site, liability limits, and key policies.

URL—address that specifies the location of a particular web page or other resource on the Internet, along with the method used to access it; short for Uniform Resource Locator.

USABILITY—ability for visitors to achieve the outcomes they seek on a digital resource.

USABILITY TEST—a test of usability by having visitors try to complete tasks and observing the results.

USE CASE—a written description of how a user will perform a task on a website, beginning with a user goal and ending when that goal is fulfilled.

USER EXPERIENCE—the emotions and attitudes a visitor has about their interactions with a digital business, including their perceptions of how usable and efficient a digital business is.

WEB ANALYTICS—the measurement, collection, and analysis of web usage data, in order to improve digital business performance.

WEB HOSTING—a service that makes web sites available on the Internet.

WEB PAGE—document written in HTML (Hyper Text Markup Language) that is suitable for displaying through a web browser. Web pages can include Style Sheet Rules and other code.

Appendices

BUSINESS GOALS AND OBJECTIVES		COMPETITORS
Type of digital business: Business objective:		Closest competitor: How will you be different or better?
ACQUISITION	**BEHAVIOR**	**CONVERSIONS**
Keyword search phrase: Visitors/month:	Available domain name: Most important use case:	Primary conversion goal: Revenue stream:
Social media platform: Content and frequency: Visitors/month:		
CONVERSION EQUATION		
Primary conversion goal: visitors/month * % conversion rate = conversions/month		

Digital Business Design Canvas v. 1.0 6/14/18 CC BY-SA 3.0 JP Allen
jpedia.org

The Road to the Prototype

Step	Task	Success Measure
1	Log on to web hosting control panel.	See your web hosting control panel on the screen.
2	Find the file directory that contains your publicly available web pages. (More advanced: set up an FTP client.)	See the contents of your public web directory on a screen (or using an FTP client).
3	Upload an image file to your web hosting account and make it available on the Internet at your own domain name.	View the image at your domain, using a web browser.
4	Upload a document, such as a PDF or Word file, to your web hosting account and make it available on the Internet at your own domain name.	View the document at your domain, using a web browser.
5	Create a web page document that includes the following html tags: title, list, link, and image. Upload the web page document to your web hosting account and make it available on the Internet at your own domain name.	View the web page at your domain, using a web browser. No broken link or image.
6	Add two style sheet rules (written in CSS) to a web page document. Upload the web page document to your web hosting account and make it available on the Internet at your own domain name.	View the web page at your domain, using a web browser. Style sheet changes are visible.

Step	Task	Success Measure
7	Install a new WordPress site on your web hosting account. Find its web address (URL).	View the new WordPress site using a web browser.
8	Log on to administrator control panel (Dashboard) of your new WordPress site.	View the Dashboard of your WordPress site in a browser.
9	Change title and tag line on WordPress site.	View site with edited title.
10	Add new content to WordPress site (one page and one post).	View page and view post in a browser.
11	Assign a category to content.	View page with all the content for a category.
12	Add an item to the main menu on WordPress site.	View changed menu in browser.
13	Set home page of WordPress site to be a page you create.	View new home page in browser at the site's URL.
14	Change the theme on your WordPress site.	View site in browser with new theme.
15	Add a new widget to your WordPress site.	View site with new widget.
16	Configure and activate a new plugin on your WordPress site.	View site with new plugin working.
17	Add a new user to your WordPress site.	View site with new user logged in.
18	Customize a style sheet rule on your WordPress site.	View site with customized style sheet rule.

Congrats! You now know just enough to be dangerous . . .

Index

Note: Page numbers in **bold** indicate a table on the corresponding page.